How I Retired By Age 45

45

Investing in Real Estate for Beginners

How I Retired By Age 45

Investing in Real Estate for Beginners

Clifford T. Wellman Jr.

How I Retired By Age 45: Investing in Real Estate for Beginners

Copyright © 2019 by Clifford T. Wellman Jr. All rights reserved.

No part of this publication may be reproduced, stored in a retrieval system or transmitted in any way by any means, electronic, mechanical, photocopy, recording or otherwise without the prior permission of the author except as provided by USA copyright law.

Published by Hidden Lodge, LLC.
cliffwellman@hotmail.com

Book design copyright © 2019 by Clifford T. Wellman Jr. All rights reserved.
Cover design by Clifford T. Wellman Jr.
Interior design by Clifford T. Wellman Jr.

Published in the United States of America

ISBN: 978-1-79319-146-5

1. Business & Economics / Investing & Securities / Real Estate
2. Business & Economics / Real Estate / Buying & Selling Homes

To my wife.
Together we began chasing our dream
and together we achieved it.
Financial Freedom could only be found
when we worked together as a team.
We never let fear stop us!

Contents

1. Why I wrote this book 7
2. How much money do you need? 8
3. What makes me different? 11
4. The cost of living 17
5. Passive Income Streams 20
6. Assets versus Liabilities 25
7. How I got started 28
8. Let's buy some houses 32
9. Taxes and Asset Protection 42
10. One more deal 47
11. Go big or go home! 54
12. Let's make a plan 64
13. How to find your first property 68
14. Building your credit score 92
15. Balance Sheets 95
16. Being Rich versus Wealthy 97
17. Managing Risk 99
18. Building a team 101
19. Where are you? 106
20. Parting Words 110

Why I wrote this book

I wrote this book so that I could share my investment story with you and possibly help you find your own path to retirement. The title comes from a dream that I shared with my father when I was 25 years old. Retiring by the age of 45 is cool, but 45 isn't a magic number. If you're 25 and you get started now, there's no reason you can't retire by the time you are 30 or 35. If you're 50 years old and you're not sure what retirement looks like for you, you can apply the information that I share in this book and retire by the time you are between 55 and 60 years old and have more money at retirement than you ever thought possible.

I hope to provide inspiration and encouragement to you so that you can succeed as well. I also want to help you avoid some of the pitfalls that can come with real estate investing if you aren't careful.

Many people in your life will tell you that you're crazy to get into rental real estate. They had a horror story or have friends who have had a horror story and they don't want it to happen to you. There will be a lot of negativity, but don't let that stop you. These people simply are afraid to look outside of their *safe* world of employment. They might tell you that having a job with a 401k is safer, but once I open your eyes, you'll realize that it isn't true. Safety comes from your ability to control your financial situation. I hope to show you that rental real estate is safer than employment and is much more fulfilling.

The biggest thing that I want to accomplish with this book is to help you not be afraid to invest in real estate. Don't let your fear, or the fear of your friends and family, keep you from achieving your dreams!

How much money do you need?

How much money do you need to retire? Go out and ask this question to a hundred people and you'll probably get a hundred different answers. This is because the answer is a personal one, and so it is different for everyone. So what is the answer? I don't know, but I can tell you how to figure it out. It's a simple formula that looks like this:

Income > or = Expenses

This is a pretty simple formula that tells us that <u>income must be greater than or equal to expenses</u>. You can complicate it all you want, but in the end, this is the answer. You need to have more money coming in than you have going out. Here are some simple definitions.

> **Income** – This is the amount of money that is put into your pocket each month. We'll talk more about income in a minute, but for now just know that income is the money coming in.

> **Expenses** – This is the amount of money that is leaving your pocket each month.

Yep, it is that simple. Well, kind of. Let's talk more about income for a minute. Today, you probably have a job that generates income. The amount of income that you generate at your job is based on how many hours you work and how much money your employer pays you per hour.

> If you make $10/hour and you work 40 hours/week, then your income is $400 per week. This is called gross income. Gross income is the money that you make before taxes are taken out and paid to the government.

"Wait. This doesn't sound like retirement if I have to work for my money," you say.

You are absolutely correct. Let's talk about a couple different types of income; earned income and passive income.

Earned Income – This is income that you earn by working. The goal in retirement is for earned income to be equal to zero, correct? Yes, because we don't want to work in retirement. Not working is one of the main reasons for retirement.

Passive Income – This is income that is received on a regular basis for little or no work. This is the type of income that we are looking for.

There is an infinite number of methods for generating passive income. The list below contains a few of those methods. We'll go into further detail later:

Dividend Income – Income earned from investments in stocks.

Rental Income – Income earned from the rental of real property or personal property.

Interest Income – Income earned from lending money.

Business Income – Income earned from a business.

Book Sales Income – Income earned by publishing written works.

So let's go back to my formula (notice that I've added the word Passive):

Passive Income > or = Expenses

When our passive income is greater than our expenses, we can retire. That is the reason you are reading this book.

The formula above allows us to have an equal amount of passive income and expenses, but in reality we want passive income to be more than expenses. So once your passive income exceeds your expenses, you can retire. Once you retire, your time is now yours to use as you wish. It's time to go to the beach, take a hike in the woods, go on a long trip across the country...the options are limitless. Well, that is only true if you have included the cost of these adventures in your *expenses*. We'll talk more about expenses a little later and I'll provide some ideas for how to budget for fun activities.

The beauty of this formula is that it is scalable. If your expenses increase, all you need to do is increase your passive income. Actually, I always tell people to increase their passive income before they increase their expenses. You'll

Clifford T. Wellman Jr.

hear this a lot from me: **"Buy an asset to pay for all your liabilities."** We'll talk about Assets and Liabilities in a later chapter.

Conclusion

The lesson that we need to learn from this chapter is that we need to stay ahead of the game by increasing our passive income before increasing our expenses.

Passive Income > or = Expenses

I want to talk more about income and expenses and we'll do that in a minute, but first let's talk about me...

What makes me different?

I don't really think that I'm exceptional, my wife might disagree, but what can I say. ☺ Seriously, there are two things that separate those that succeed in retiring early and those that don't.

- Turn your dreams into goals
- Don't let fear stop you

Everyone has dreams, but if you want to retire early, you need to turn your dreams into goals.

Turn your dreams into goals

When I was 25 years old, I told my dad that I was going to retire by the time I was 45. Honestly, at that time I had no idea how I was going to do it. It was only a dream and it took me another ten years to actually turn the dream into a goal. I look back now and realize how much time I wasted. If I had turned that dream into a goal when I was 25, the title of this book might have been "How I Retired By Age 35." But I don't have regrets. I believe things happen for a reason and I'm still pretty happy that I achieved my dream of retiring by the time I was 45. I actually retired about 6 weeks before my 45th birthday.

So let's talk more about goals. Goals are really only dreams until you do two very important things:

> **Write it down** – The first thing that you need to do is write down your goal. I write mine in big letters on an 8.5" x 11" piece of paper and tape them to the wall above my computer in my home office. So every time I sit down, I am reminded of my goal. Your dream only starts to become a goal after you write it down.

> **Make a plan** – the second, and possibly more important, thing to do is to develop a plan for achieving your goal. This also has to be written down in excruciating detail. The more detail the better. There is a complete chapter later on how to write a plan. For now, just know that the more

detailed your plan is, the better chance you have of successfully completing it.

Share your goal – Yeah, I know I said that there were only two things. This third thing is optional, but I find that if I share my goals with friends and family, then I am more apt to complete them.

I have a lot of friends who work daily for someone else. Some of them really enjoy their jobs, while some of them don't. Some wish that they had more time to do other things, like spending time with family, reading a book, or exercising. But work just seems to get in the way of all the fun stuff that we'd like to do. Many people work 40 hours or more a week. I know that there were several years that I put 60-80 hours in each week. When you are working that much time, there's no time for anything else.

You probably know that there are 168 hours in a seven day week. 120 of those hours are during the "work" week. One of the things that I hated the most when I was working a job, was the amount of time that I spent commuting. I remember driving an hour or more to and from work every day, sometimes six days a week. So a normal person might spend ten hours each week commuting. Then there's sleep. I love to sleep and nowadays I get about eight hours a day, but back when I was working so much I didn't get that much. Studies have shown that lack of sleep is bad for your health. So let's say we are shooting for eight hours of sleep every night. We have to add some time for breakfast and dinner. Hopefully, you have time for such things. And if you have children who attend school, then it is very probable that you spend all of your spare time taking your children to and from a variety of after school activities.

Here is a breakdown of that time.

- 40 hours at the job
- 10 hours commuting to and from the job
- 40 hours sleeping (8 hours a night)
- 5-10 hours eating (breakfast and dinner)
- 5 hours getting ready for work
- That leaves 15-20 hours. If you are working 60+ hours a week, than most of these additional hours are gone.

The point is, when we spend so much time working and commuting, we end up not having time for ourselves or our families.

Excuses

The person who really wants to do something FINDS a way; the others just find an EXCUSE!

Excuses are simply a way for a person to rationalize why they do or don't do something. Excuses keep people from realizing their dreams. I find this to be true when I talk to people about how to retire sooner than later. Let's have a little dialog.

"So why do people spend so much time working?" I ask.

"Gotta pay the bills," you reply.

"Sure, but why work?" I ask.

"If I don't work, then I won't have money to pay the bills. Duh," you answer, starting to get frustrated because you have to repeat yourself.

I smile a little and then say, "But, what if I told you that you can earn money without working?"

"You aren't going to try to get me to join one of those pyramid schemes are you?" you ask.

At that point I laugh out loud and say, "No, but I would like to teach you how to generate passive income."

The conversation goes back and forth for a while and as I start talking about the various types of passive income streams, the person that I'm talking to almost always stops me and says one of two things:

"You need money to make money, and I don't have any money."

OR

"That sounds too risky."

Clifford T. Wellman Jr.

I don't have any money

I can relate to this statement. I'm sure that I've said it in the past, but I think that it is mostly based in fear and lack of knowledge about money. Don't get me wrong, having money definitely helps you to make more money and it is true that you do need money to make money. But who says that the money has to be yours? I started this game with zero money, but I'm getting ahead of myself. We'll come back to me in a minute. First, let's talk about the second response, "That sounds too risky".

That sounds too risky!

Boy, have I heard that a lot! This comes from a fearful mindset. Risk can be managed with education. I'm not talking about college, I'm talking about educating yourself on the aspects of rental real estate. You are educating yourself when you read this book and others like it. Anyway, I have an entire chapter on how to identify and mitigate risk later in this book. So we'll talk more about risk later.

The problem with both of these responses is that they have negative overtones, and that, my friends, is what this chapter is about.

What makes me different?

I know from experience that, even if you have nothing, you can still get started in the investment game. How do I know this? Because I had zero money when I got started. I also know how to identify and mitigate risk. I didn't let these fears stop me in the past and don't let them stop me from achieving my current goals.

I was scared as hell when I bought my first "investment property." I had no idea what I was doing, but I knew that it was the first step toward achieving my goal. I didn't have money and I didn't know anything about risk mitigation. I didn't know anything about rehabbing houses either!

My first investment property was a small, three bedroom "fixer-upper" house. It was bank owned and I was able to purchase it for $20,000. At the time, $20,000 was an insane amount of money for me to spend (to risk) on an investment. I had to borrow the down payment money and the bank lent me the rest. I put in a lot of blood, sweat, and tears into that house and then sold it for $70,000. By the way, there was literally blood, sweat, and tears involved with that fixer-upper project. So much, that I almost quit and vowed to never do it again. Well, I didn't quit and I ended up buying many more fixer-uppers over the years. As I write this, I'm actually working on another.

"Wait, I thought you were retired," you say.

"Yeah, I am, but I want to buy a toy and as I've said in the past, *buy an asset to pay for all your liabilities*." In this case, replace the word "liabilities" with the word "toy". Besides, I still enjoy turning something that is ugly into something that is pretty, and of course, there's the money.

There are risks in everything that we do. It's just a matter of identifying and mitigating the risk and knowing how much risk you can handle. The beautiful thing about the risks that I take while investing, is that I am able to control most of the risk. Yes, there are things outside of my control, but for the most part, I am in control. In the case of a single family home, I decide where the house will be. I decide what type of house to buy. I decided how much money I will spend. There will be expenses that I can't anticipate, there always are, but you can include a chunk of money for "unknown expenses" in your budget. Whether I decide to sell or rent, I get to set the rent amount and the sale price. Of course you have to know the market that you are in, because the rent amount and sale price are all constrained by the market, but I still get to control those numbers. If I need to sell a house for $20,000 above what the market will bear, then I won't be buying that house.

As an employee, we are dependent on our employer for our job. I could be one of the best workers in the business and still lose my job because the rest of the company is falling apart. If the employer decides to downsize, I could lose my job. If the employer decides to close up shop, I could lose my job. If the employer sells the business, I could lose my job. I get paid what the employer says I get paid. Sure I can negotiate, but in the end, the control is with the employer. I could argue that it is riskier to be employed than it is to be generating passive income on your own, but let's not fight about it.

Conclusion

So *What makes me different?* At the beginning, I said there were two things that make me different. The first is that I realize my dreams by turning them into goals. I then create a plan for accomplishing my goals. The plan contains very detailed steps and action items. I develop strategies for identifying and mitigating risk. The second thing is, I don't let fear keep me from realizing my dreams.

Don't let fear dictate who you are or what you can possibly be!

Don't let other people's fear dictate who you are or what you can possibly be!

Dream big! Set goals! Create a plan! And don't let fear stop you!!

The cost of living

In order to retire, one of the first things you need to figure out is how much money you spend each month. It is this number that tells you how much passive income you need to generate each month in order for you to retire. So, let's make a list of all your expenses. I've created a sample list below:

Mortgage/Rent	$700
Car Payment	$300
Car Insurance	$100
Electricity	$ 60
Gas (heating)	$ 85
Water/Sewer	$ 45
Telephone	$ 50
Cable TV	$100
Internet	$ 60
Life Insurance Premium	$100
Food	$300
Miscellaneous	$100
Gas (for car)	$100
Credit Cards	$100
Savings	$100
Monthly Total	**$2,300**

This list is only a start. It is a great exercise for you to create a list like this of your own monthly bills. If you can't do this readily, then I recommend that you spend the next month recording every penny that you spend and organizing it into a list similar to the one above. If you don't know how much money you are spending every month, then you are probably spending every penny that you have.

In the list above, I included an item that most people don't always include in their list and that item is *Savings*. Every month you should be putting some money into a savings account. We'll cover this topic a little later when I talk about investing and increasing your passive income. I like to think that a savings account is sort of like paying myself money. Notice that with all of the other items above, you are paying someone else. You work hard, you should pay yourself. You might ask, "What is this savings for?" That is a good question. Savings can be for several things; emergencies, special events, vacations, new toys, etc. Actually, if you have specific things that you want to spend money on, I recommend creating a line item in the list for that item. I also recommend that you always have an emergency savings account.

Okay, so according to our list above, you need to make at least $2,300 a month in passive income in order to "retire". Personally, I would probably add an additional $500 a month to that, so that I always have a surplus.

Let's talk about some of those special line items above. Maybe you have been looking at a fun toy, like a pontoon boat or a snowmobile. There are two ways to purchase a toy like this. <u>Never</u> go into debt when buying a toy. There is one exception to that rule and we'll go through that in a minute. The first way to buy your toy is to save for that toy. Once you have saved enough money to purchase your toy, go out and pay for it with cash. Paying for a large item with cash is satisfying. You really feel like you've accomplished something when you do that. The next way to purchase the item is to finance it.

"Uh, wait, I thought you said not to go into debt," you say.

Yes, I did say that, but there is one way that you can finance it without it negatively affecting your retirement plan. If you do it correctly, it will actually improve your retirement plan.

"So how do I finance my toy without it negatively affecting my retirement plan?" you ask.

The answer is "Purchase an Asset."

"Purchase an asset?" you ask.

Yes, we'll go into detail about assets in another chapter, but for now consider this. Let's say you want to buy a snowmobile that costs $15,000. It will take most people a long time to save $15,000. We live in a world that expects instant gratification, so how can you be expected to wait? There are instances where waiting is actually the best course of action, but let's say in this case you just can't wait. A good friend of mine always calls me "Mr. Patience." Yeah, I'm not really a patient person, so he was picking on me. I always want what I want, when I want it, and not a minute later. He would probably disagree, but I have actually learned to be patient over the years, at least to some degree.

Enough about me. So this snowmobile can be financed for $250 per month with zero money down. Your current budget (from a few pages back) doesn't support this new expense. So how can we buy it? The short answer is that we need to create more (passive) income. So let's say that we buy a rental property that will generate $300 a month in passive income. This income covers the $250 payment on the snowmobile and also puts $50 in your pocket each month. Sounds like a good deal and in 5 or 6 years when the snowmobile is paid off, this new asset will be putting $300 into your pocket each month, instead of $50. Now this deal sounds even better.

There are "experts" out there who tell us to live below our means. They say that we should budget our money so that we spend less than we make. In general, that is true, but it is also very limiting. One thing I learned from Robert Kiyosaki (the author of *Rich Dad Poor Dad*) was that we don't need to live below our means, we need to increase our means to live the way we want. *Rich Dad Poor Dad* is an excellent book that I recommend to everyone.

That rental house that I mentioned above is a form of passive income. A lot of people have horror stories about rental real estate. I have a few, but I wouldn't let that stop you from taking advantage of this passive income stream. If you do it right, you can do it in any real estate market. We'll touch on real estate a little later as well, but first let's talk more about passive income.

Conclusion

First, you need to determine how much you spend every month. These expenses determine how much passive income you need to generate each month. Don't forget to include a *Savings* line item in your list of expenses.

Passive Income Streams

In the second chapter, I listed a few passive income streams. That is definitely not an exhaustive list. I'm sure there are things that could be on that list that I've never even considered, but I will walk you through the streams that I listed, to get you thinking.

Dividend Income

Dividend income comes from stocks. Just so you know, not all stocks pay a dividend. Dividends are paid periodically, most often quarterly, and the amount that they pay is generally affected by the value of the stock. If the stock value goes up, the dividend per share tends to go down a bit. Let's say a stock is paying $1 per share, per quarter. If you have 50 shares, then you'll get paid a dividend of $50 for that quarter. Simple enough, right? The rate of return on your money is actually pretty low when you only consider the dividend income that you are making. Let's say each share costs you $100 and you have 50 shares, then your total investment is $5,000. If you are making $200 a year in dividend income ($50 per quarter), then your rate of return is only 4%. The rate of return is calculated by taking the income ($200) and dividing it by the investment ($5,000). Granted, 4% is better than the 0.5% that you might make with that same $5,000 in a savings account, but in the grand scheme of things, this rate of return is not very good. Now I'm not saying that investing in this stock was a bad idea, because what if the value of the stock goes up? Let's say in 12 months the value went up to $150. The stock is now worth $7,500 (50 @ $150). That is a gain of $2,500. If we add the dividend income of $200, our annual gain is now $2,700 or 54% on your money. Now that is looking way better. But conversely, what if the value of the stock goes down to $80 and is now valued at $4,000 (50 @ $80). You've lost $1,000 and with the dividend gain of $200, your loss is $800. That's not good. I consider stocks very risky because you have virtually zero control of the investment. The stock market can be good place to invest if you know what you're doing. Education is key. If you decided to invest in the stock market, educate yourself.

Rental Income

Rental Income can come from either real property or personal property. Real property is land and buildings. Personal property is things like equipment, automobiles, or toys like boats, RVs, snowmobiles, etc. I have never dabbled in the rental of personal property, so I won't be talking about it here. I'm sure there is money to be made, because a lot of businesses do it. Mobile homes are considered personal property, but for the purposes of this book, I will include them in the real property section.

Real property can be commercial or residential. I'm sure some people might want to add industrial property to this list, but for simplicity I'm including it with commercial. Commercial, for our purposes, is renting real property to a business. Residential is real property rented to people living at the property. There really isn't much difference between commercial and residential when you look at the numbers. The key to *Rental Income* is cash flow. Cash flow is the surplus money left over after all expenses have been paid. Let's look at our rental house we discussed in the previous chapter. Right now we are only talking about financials related to cash flow and not how we purchased the property.

Monthly Income and Expenses	
Rental Income	$800 (paid by tenant)
Taxes	$100
Insurance	$ 50
Mortgage	$300
Maintenance	$ 50
Total Expenses	$500
Cash flow	$300 (surplus cash)

In this case, we own a residential property in which a tenant pays $800 per month in rent. The tenant is responsible for all utilities, so that is not part of these numbers. If the utilities are included in the rent, then we would include them as expenses in this list. We would also take that into consideration when determining what the rent amount will be. We'll talk more about how to purchase this house a little later.

Clifford T. Wellman Jr.

Interest Income

Interest income is money that you earn from interest. This might be the 0.5% interest you earn on the money that you have in your savings account. It could also be the 1.5% that you are getting from money that you have in a money market account. *Experts* would considered these types of savings accounts as a "risk free" investment strategy, except when you consider that the rate of inflation is higher than the interest that these products are providing. If you take inflation into account, you are actually losing money when you keep it in the bank. Okay, that might be a little harsh, but it is true. The one reason for keeping your money in a bank or credit union, is that your money is liquid. By liquid, I mean that it is readily accessible and spendable.

There are other types of interest that you can earn. Consider this: if you buy a car and get a loan from the bank, then you are paying the bank interest. Maybe 3-5% depending on your credit score. If you buy a home or get a commercial loan for a business, you might pay a bank 5-7% in interest. Obviously, these rates are always changing, so make sure you know what the current rates are before you make any decisions. If the bank is lending money and generating interest income, then why can't you? Well, you can. The rules change all the time, so make sure that you stay on top of the laws if you ever decide to lend your money. Individuals who lend money are called *hard money* lenders. These individuals will charge an interest rate anywhere from 7% to 25%.

"25%!!!! Are you serious?" you ask.

Yup, one of the main reasons people use hard money lenders is because they can't get the money anywhere else. If you use a hard money lender, always make sure it is for a short term, no more than 12-18 months. Most of them will want their money back by then anyway. The great thing about hard money lenders, is that they provide you a way to purchase a business or rental property, when you couldn't have otherwise done so. So paying their high interest rate for a short time, will make it worth it. Hey, if it isn't worth it in the end, then you shouldn't borrow the money. Obviously, I'm not talking about a loan shark who is going to send over his guy to break your legs when you haven't paid back the money on time.

Business Income

Creating a business can be very fruitful and satisfying. The thing that I enjoy most about creating a business is the idea that I am helping other people. How am I helping people? First, a business provides a product or service that people want and/or need. Second, businesses employ people. Statistics show that people who are employed are happier than those who are not.

For a business, the key word is once again, *cash flow*. Cash flow of a business is calculated the same way it is done with rental income.

Revenue – Expenses = Cash flow (income)

Revenue is the money collected from customers for the product or service that is being provided by the business. Depending on the product or service, there are a variety of expenses associated with the revenue that is generated. The idea is to make sure that the resulting income is greater than zero. Another word for cash flow in a business is **Net Operating Income** (NOI). We'll talk more about NOI later as well.

Be careful that you don't let your business turn into a job. Your business isn't generating passive income if you have to show up to work every day. You should be able to stay away from the day to day business activities and let your managers run everything. If the business continues to thrive without you running the show, then it is truly a passive income business. If you have to be there day to day, then it's really just a job and you are not retired.

Income from Book Sales

Why did I separate Book Sales from Business Income? I separated this because, as an author, you create a book once and sell it many times. Publishing books has become incredibly easy in the last five years or so. I am fairly new to the book writing business. Actually, I never really considered writing a book until a few years ago. My first book is a work of fiction. It is a fictional thriller that is based on Biblical prophecy titled, *The Road to Revelation – The Beginning*. It is the first in a series. The second in the series, *The Road to Revelation – World at War*, was just published as I'm writing this. It is funny, but those two books are the reason I wrote this one. I

Clifford T. Wellman Jr.

was explaining to someone about the books that I wrote and also about my real estate investment history, and he said that I should write a book about investing. So here we are. Not everyone will have designs to write a book. Like I said, I never did, but each of us has specialized knowledge about something. Maybe it's time that you shared that knowledge with the world. It is the information age after all.

Conclusion

Passive income gives us the means for living the life that we always wanted to live. One of the dreams that I've had for as long as I can remember was to purchase 100 acres of land. I wanted this land to be covered in trees and it would eventually be a place where I would live, hunt, and thrive. I recently bought my 100 acre wood, actually 120 acres, and it included a log cabin. The cool thing is that I bought it with cash. Sure, I could have financed it, but as I said in the beginning, there is a certain amount of satisfaction in paying for something with cash.

With all that said, I'd like to talk about rental real estate, but first we need to discuss the difference between an asset and a liability.

Assets versus Liabilities

One of the most important things you can learn is the difference between an asset and a liability. Assets and liabilities are the primary pieces that we use to build our balance sheet. Banks love balance sheets, because it gives them a clear picture of the health of your business. For the purpose of this chapter, we will think about assets in two different ways. The first is in regards to cash flow and the other is in regards to net worth. Liabilities are treated basically the same regardless. All liabilities take money out of your pocket.

Cash flow

Simply put, when thinking about cash flow, an asset is something that puts money into your pocket. Things like your house, your car, and your other expensive toys aren't part of this asset equation. The primary reason for this is that these things don't put money into your pocket, however the debt associated with them is still a liability because they actually take money out of your pocket and reduce your cash flow. Having debt on these things is generally not a good idea and I consider this bad debt. As I said, in a previous chapter, the one exception to this is when you purchase an income generating asset that pays for the debt associated with these toys.

Good debt is associated with an *asset* that generates income.

Bad debt is associated with an *asset* that doesn't generate income.

Let's look at this example;

You buy a 3 bedroom home that you rent out to a tenant for $800 a month. The value of the home is $80,000. The total amount of debt that you have on the home is $50,000. The associated expenses related to this home are $500 a month. From a cash flow point of view this property generated $300 of cash flow each month. Using the cash flow formula from the previous chapter:

Revenue – Expenses = Cash flow (income)

So, $800 (rent) - $500 (expenses) = $300 cash flow.

Clifford T. Wellman Jr.

Net Worth

Simply put, net worth is the value of your assets less your liabilities. In this calculation, we include things like your house, your car, and your boat. So let's look at our example again in regards to net worth. In this case, the asset is valued at $80,000 and the liability (mortgage) is $50,000. Net worth is calculated using the following formula:

value of asset – amount of liability = Net worth

So, $80,000 - $50,000 = $30,000 net worth.

Let's take the same home and say that you are living in it instead of renting it. The only change we'll have is that you aren't collecting $800 in rent. Here is what we get:

Revenue – Expenses = Cash flow (income)

So, $0 (rent) - $500 (expenses) = $-500 (negative cash flow)

value of asset – amount of liability = Net worth

So, $80,000 - $50,000 = $30,000 net worth.

We see that from a *net worth* point of view, your home that you live in is still an asset, but from a *cash flow* point of view it is not, because you'll never get income from it as long as you are living in it. One exception, you could include your personal residence as a *cash flow* asset if you rented out a portion of your home to someone else. If you apply the same logic to your car, boat, snowmobile, etc., you'll see that these things are not assets when we think about cash flow. However, when you are filling out a loan application for a bank, the bank wants you to include these items because they will consider them as part of your net worth. Banks will view all of these assets as a way to determine if you can pay back a loan by liquidating assets if you ever quit making your monthly loan payments.

Another example

Let's go back to the idea of buying a rental to cover the costs of a snowmobile. We'll use the same house that we used above, and the value of the snowmobile was $15,000 and the monthly payment was $250. For the sake of this example, let's assume that you put $3,000 down on the snowmobile when you bought it, so your loan is $12,000.

The Numbers:	
Snowmobile value	$15,000 (asset)
Snowmobile loan	$12,000 (liability)
Snowmobile net worth	$3,000 (value - loan)
Snowmobile payment	$250 / month
Home value	$80,000 (asset)
Home loan	$50,000 (liability)
Home net worth	$30,000 (value - loan)
Home expenses	$500 (includes taxes and insurance)
Home rent	$800 (paid by tenant)
Home cash flow	$300 (rent - expenses)

Cash flow calculation:
  Home cash flow - snowmobile payment = Total cash flow
  $300 - $250 = $50

Net worth calculation:
  Home net worth + snowmobile net worth = Total net worth
  $30,000 + $3,000 = $33,000

Hopefully you can see how assets are treated when we are talking about cash flow versus when we are talking about net worth.

Conclusion

It is important to know how assets and liabilities are treated when calculating cash flow and net worth.

How I got started

I already told you about my first fixer-upper, but I only gave you a glimpse. In this chapter, I will talk to you about buying single family homes that you'll turn into rental income (passive income). I'll show you how to find the best deals and I'll show you how to look at a house and quickly determine if it is a deal worth doing.

When buying a rental property, you first must determine its **After Repair Value** (ARV). This is the value of a property after it has been remodeled to a reasonable standard. This value will be based on the condition of the house as well as on the market that the house is in. So let's use the rental house mentioned in previous chapters as our example. We've already determined the value of the house to be $80,000. This is the ARV. But let's roll back the clock to the time before we purchased the house. Let's say the house was a bank owned foreclosure that needed a fair amount of work and you can purchase it for $30,000. After doing a quick walk through of the house, you determine that you'll need to do about $20,000 in repairs to bring the value back up to $80,000. So after we've purchased the house and fixed it up, our total investment will be $50,000. With a value of $80,000, that gives us $30,000 in equity. Equity is calculated similarly to the way we calculated net worth in the previous chapter.

> **Value - Investment = Equity**

For example, $80,000 - $50,000 = $30,000.

Before you ever decide to buy a property, you need to understand how much equity you'll have when it is fixed up. You'll use this equity number as a way to quickly determine if you want to buy the house. I can literally walk into a house and usually within 20 to 30 minutes I know where I will be once it is all fixed up. Additionally, you'll also want to know what kind of cash flow the property will generate. You have to understand your *housing market* as well as your *rental market* before you'll be able to quickly make these calculations. Having a realtor that knows both markets will help you tremendously. Find a good realtor before you get started.

At this point, you need to determine your exit strategy. You have two choices: Do you want to buy the house, fix it up and sell it or do you want to buy the house, fix it up and rent it? Selling it will put cash in your pocket now, renting it will generate cash flow (passive income) over time.

Let's look at each version of this deal.

Buy-Sell Deal (Exit Strategy 1)

The Numbers (Buying)	
Purchase Price	$30,000
Repairs	$20,000
Total Costs	$50,000
20% Down payment	$10,000 (initial investment)
Mortgage Amount	$40,000

The Numbers (Selling)	
Sale Price (ARV)	$80,000
Less Closing Costs	$ 8,000 (approximately 10% of Sale Price)
Less Total Costs	$50,000 (from above)
Cash Earned	$22,000

The **cash on cash return** (COCR) for this deal is 220%!

Cash Earned ÷ Initial Investment = COCR
$22,000 ÷ $10,000 = 220%

The nice thing about this Buy-Sell deal is that you have cash at the end to buy your next property. **Cash on cash return** is a term commonly used by investors. Since it is dependent on the initial investment, you can really increase the COCR if you are able to take advantage of *other people's money*!

Later in this book, I will give you examples where I bought houses with no money down. I will show you some cases where I got a check at close when I bought a property.

Clifford T. Wellman Jr.

We'll use all the same numbers from above, with the exception of the closing costs, which you won't have until you sell the property.

Buy-Rent Deal (Exit Strategy 2)

The Numbers (Buying)	
Purchase Price	$30,000
Repairs	$20,000
Total Costs	$50,000
20% Down payment	$10,000 (initial investment)
Mortgage Amount	$40,000

The Numbers (Renting)	
Monthly Rent	$ 800
Monthly Expenses	$ 500
Monthly Cashflow	$ 300
Annual Cashflow	$3,600

Annual Cash flow ÷ Initial Investment = Annual Return on Investment
$3,600 ÷ $10,000 = 36%

The beauty of this deal is that you are making 36% annually and will have recouped your initial investment in less than 3 years.

In both of these examples, we provided 20% down payment on the mortgage on the house, which included both the purchase price and the repairs. You can do better, if you get creative.

Let's go back to my first investment property.

My first investment property

The Numbers (Selling)	
Sale Price (ARV)	$70,000
Less Closing Costs	$ 7,000 (approximately 10% of Sale Price)
Less Purchase Price	$20,000
Less Repair Costs	$20,000
Cash at Close	$23,000

In this deal, I didn't have any money to use as a down payment, so I got help from my parents for the down payment which was only 10% or $4,000. The remaining $36,000 was a mortgage. Not all banks will give you money to do repairs on a home, but if the property will appraise for the amount of the loan before the repairs are made, then there is a chance.

This particular house was a bank owned foreclosure at the time. The bank didn't want it on their books, so they were happy to sell it to me knowing that I was going to fix it up and sell it. This was in 2003, before the real estate bubble popped in 2007.

If you consider my initial investment of $0, my cash on cash return was infinite. That is pretty cool. Even better, after I sold the house, I had $23,000 in cash!! You may recall that I told you before that I vowed never to do another fixer-upper again. I had so many unexpected problems with this property that I almost kept my word on that vow. Frankly, I chose the wrong house to be my first fixer-upper. There was just too much work to do. I had a full time job and did all of the work myself. Talk about not having any free time. It was another *four* years before I bought another investment property.

Conclusion

Before you buy a property, know your housing market as well as your rental market. Determine the After Repair Value (ARV) to see if the property is worth your time. Know your exit strategy. Are you are going to sell the property after fixing it up or are you going to rent it? Calculating the Cash on Cash Return of a property will help you determine if the property is a good buy. It also can help you determine your exit strategy.

Let's buy some houses

As I said in the previous chapter, it was a full four years before I got back into the real estate investment game. Four years is a long time. Why did I come back? I came back because I knew that I needed to get back at it if I wanted to retire by the time I was 45. I was getting tired of my existing career at the time.

I started in the software development world in 1990. I went from developing Windows applications, to web development, to project management, and finally to management. In 2003, right before I purchased by first fixer-upper, I had just been fired from my job as a Director of Internet Development. At the time, I managed a team of 40-50 people and it was a very time consuming job. It turned out not to be a good fit for me. My boss and I just didn't see eye to eye and there was a lot of stress on both sides. I'm not ashamed of getting fired, because it ended up being the best thing that ever happened to me. Don't get me wrong, it hurt me financially. I took about an $80,000 pay cut! I had been on the management path for about five years, and in that time my software development skills had become a little rusty.

So here I am, unemployed and not really sure what I want to do with my life. I knew that I didn't want to go back to management, and I was a little behind the current development technologies. So I rolled up my sleeves and learned the new development technologies and got started.

"What the heck does all that have to do with buying houses?" you ask.

The point of the story is that I just took the worst financial hit of my life and was kind of down on my luck. Not only did I have to start a new career in software development (basically at the bottom), I had also decided to work on the fixer-upper that I talked about in the previous chapter. Starting two new careers at the same time proved to be far too stressful, so after the first fixer-upper being so painful, sticking to what I knew best, software development, was the path I chose. That is why it took me four years to get back in the real estate investment game.

Additionally, because I had lost my job in 2003 and took a huge pay cut, I was forced to sell a house that I could no longer afford and move to a smaller town where I could find a house within my price range. I ended up moving to a small town in central Michigan.

So let's run the clock forward to 2007. The housing market had begun to free fall and people were losing their homes to foreclosure. Banks had far too many foreclosed homes on their books. It was the perfect storm. So one day, I'm sitting in my office working on a software project and my wife comes in and says that there is a workshop by some guy named Robert Kiyosaki. It turns out that he's not actually doing the workshop, but it is run by his company. I agree to go, and we sit through the 60 minute sales pitch. Honestly, they provided some pretty good information during those 60 minutes, enough that we decided to attend a weekend conference a few weeks later. I think we spent $150 on the conference and probably another $150 on the hotel. My $300 investment ended up being well worth it. During that conference, we were given more tools and ideas on how to make money in rental real estate. That weekend was all that we needed to get us back into the real estate investment game.

I started buying books and attending classes on real estate investing. You may recall earlier that I recommended educating yourself if you are going to invest in anything. This is what I'm talking about. Educate yourself and you'll be ahead of the game.

So after my wife and I started educating ourselves, we decided that it was time to get started on our retirement plan. The first thing we did was find a good realtor. Then we started looking at homes. I spent a lot of time using websites like realtor.com and zillow.com to find potential properties. Those tools are great to find properties and to see what is for sale and selling in your market, but a good realtor will help you far better than any of those sites. A realtor can put you on an automated email system that will send you new listings that meet your criteria. This way you see homes that are available when they come on the market. Sometimes you'll even get a heads up before they come on the market.

Let's look at my first investment home since the reboot.

Clifford T. Wellman Jr.

House #1

My realtor started showing us houses right away. Oh wait! It is a good idea to get with a bank or credit union and get preapproved before you spend too much time looking at houses. It is a real bummer when you find a great house but then can't get the financing. So establishing relationships with local banks is a good idea.

Anyway, a few weeks after getting started we put in an offer on our first investment property. It was pretty exciting and a little nerve racking. The home that we put an offer on was bank owned and after a little negotiations we came to the agreed price of $39,000 for a nice sized 3 bedroom, 1 bathroom house.

A little side note, by this time (2007), I had successfully reintegrated myself into the software development world and as a consultant I was making more money than when I was a Director of Internet Development. But as you might know, the more money you make, the more money you spend, and if you don't create a budget for yourself, you'll spend every penny. At this time in my life, I still hadn't learned this lesson. I did have some money put aside, but not as much as I should have. However, the one thing that I did have was a great credit rating. We'll talk more about credit later, but for now just know that banks loved to give me money. Even though the housing market was in a free fall I was still able to get a 100% loan for the $52,000 on the house.

"Wait, I thought you said that you bought it for $39,000?" you ask.

Yes, I did, but the house appraised for $75,000 and the bank was willing to give me an additional $13,000 for repairs. We ended up only spending about $5,000 on repairs and rented it almost immediately for $800 a month. My loan payment was $377. In order to determine cash flow on this property we need to add taxes, insurance, and maintenance to the list of expenses. One thing that I should mention is that before buying this property, I already had a good idea what the income and expenses would be, so I had a real good idea what type of cash flow I should be getting each month. Always know these numbers before you make the offer. Remember it's all about control!

Let's take a look at the numbers for house #1.

The Numbers (Purchase)	
ARV	$75,000
Purchase Price	$39,000
Mortgage	$52,000 (just under 70% of ARV)
Initial investment	$0 (the Mortgage was > Purchase Price)
Cash at Close	$13,000 (Mortgage - Purchase Price)
Less Repair Costs	$ 5,000
Cash in Pocket	$ 8,000 (Cash at Close - Repair Costs)

The Numbers (Rental)	
Monthly Rent	$800
Mortgage	$377
Insurance	$ 75
Taxes	$150
Maintenance	$ 28
Total Expenses	$630
Monthly Cash flow	$170 (Rent - Total Expenses)
Annual Cash flow	$2,040

With an initial investment of $0, here was another infinite return. But notice that I also got $8,000 in cash from the deal. $13,000 from the bank less the $5,000 spent on repairs. I got cash and cash flow all in one deal. This type of deal is still possible even in 2019 as I write this book, you just have to find them.

Okay, so I bought my first cash flow property. Now what do I do? Well, I was hungry for more, so even before we were done getting this house ready to rent, I was looking for more.

Houses #2, 3, 4 &5

As I mentioned earlier, by this time I had developed a good relationship with a local realtor who was also an investor. At the time he had 15-20 properties. Later in his career, he moved up to multi-unit properties, like apartments, and had somewhere around 250 units before he decided to retire. I also

Clifford T. Wellman Jr.

established relationships with several local banks. I prefer local banks versus big banks, because they give you personalized service. I love credit unions too. They love to lend money.

After having our first successful investment property under our belt, we decided to look for more. As I said, I was building relationships with local banks and through one of these relationships, I got a lead on a house that they had foreclosed on. The lead was on a nice house that they were willing to sell for $35,000. This was house #2. My wife and I looked at the property and decided to put an offer on it. For some reason it took the bank a very long time to approve the offer. If I remember correctly, it was a couple months before we finally heard back from them.

In the mean time, my wife and I kept looking for other investment properties. My realtor helped us find the next house. We walked through the property and put in an offer. The seller was a little quirky and it took us a long time to come to an agreement on this house as well, but in the end, we agreed to $28,000. This was house #3. This deal ended up dragging its feet and I wasn't sure if it would ever close.

Because I wasn't really a patient person, I continued looking for our next investment property. With the help of my realtor, I found two houses that were being sold by an estate. There are a couple of things that I liked about them. First, they were already being rented by long term tenants. Second, they were right next to each other, so maintenance could be streamlined. But the seller was asking $90,000 for both homes. That is $45,000 each, which is way more than I spent on my first property. It was also more than both of the other two offers that we had outstanding. Anyway, I liked them, but I wasn't super excited about them so I gave them a low ball offer. They wanted $90,000 for both and I offered $60,000. These were houses #4 & #5. As I said, they were both being rented by long term tenants, but the rent amounts were lower than market averages at that time. However, at $60,000 I could still do pretty good on them. The seller ended up countering at $80,000. For some reason, I was out of town for a few weeks and I didn't have a chance to respond to their counter offer. That was when the funniest thing happened. They countered their counter with $72,000. I decided to accept their second counter offer, knowing that I would immediately have cash flow on both properties.

Note to self: Always look for motivated sellers. If you find a seller who is motivated, you can always get a good deal. This seller was an estate and the children of the older couple that had owned them didn't want to continue renting them. It was easier for them to just sell the houses.

A little sidebar about real estate investment properties; When you are buying investment properties, don't get emotional about it. The deal has to be about the numbers and only the numbers. I don't care if it's cute or whatever. You are never going to live in it, so don't get emotional. If the seller doesn't like your offer, walk away...there's a chance that they'll come after you.

Holy cow what did we just do?

Okay, so now I have three offers out on four houses. These offers were extended to the sellers, over a period of a couple months, and the craziest thing happened. They all came back ready to close, all in the same week. Okay, I know that I said that banks loved me, but buying four investment properties in the same week may be pushing the envelope a bit. Do you recall me saying that I was scared as hell buying my first house? Imagine me now. Fortunately, house #2 needed virtually no work and would rent fast. House #3 needed a lot of work, including a roof, but I had recently found a good crew to do that type of work. Houses #4 & #5 were already rented and would cash flow immediately. So let's talk about each deal individually.

House #2

House #2 was a bank foreclosure and we agreed to a sale price of $35,000. I approached my credit union for a loan and they were interested. House #2 ended up appraising for $70,000, and the bank was willing to loan me up to 80% of the value, which was $56,000. With a price of $35,000, that left me with $21,000 for repairs. It turned out that I only needed about $5,000 for repairs, and just like that, I put $16,000 into my pocket. It's awesome going to a closing where you are buying a house and getting a big check too. You may recall that I had done a similar thing with house #1, where I put $8,000 into my pocket.

Let's take a look at the numbers for house #2.

The Numbers (Purchase)	
ARV	$70,000
Purchase Price	$35,000
Mortgage	$56,000 (80% of ARV)
Initial investment	$0 (the Mortgage was > Purchase Price)
Cash at Close	$21,000 (Mortgage - Purchase Price)
Less Repair Costs	$ 5,000
Cash in Pocket	$16,000 (Cash at Close - Repair Costs)

The Numbers (Rental)	
Monthly Rent	$700
Mortgage	$333
Insurance	$ 67
Taxes	$100
Maintenance	$ 50
Total Expenses	$550
Monthly Cash flow	$150 (Rent - Total Expenses)
Annual Cash flow	$1,800

House #3

I chose a different path for financing house #3. I didn't want to use the cash that I had from the closings on house #1 and #2 as a down payment on house #3, because I knew that I would need some of it for houses #4 & #5. So I contacted a hard money lender that I knew through a friend. I told him that I needed $35,000 and that I needed it for 6 months. The terms were 12% interest and I wouldn't pay any interest until the end of the term (6 months). Twelve percent is a lot, but in the big picture, it was only for a short period of time and it allowed me to buy the house when I was already pushing the limits with the banks. This house was being purchased for $28,000 and pretty much all of the remaining $7,000 would be put into the house in the form of repairs. Once the house was repaired and appraised, I was able to get a loan with the credit union for $50,000.

"Wait, what? $50,000?" you ask.

Yep, I did it again. The house appraised for $62,500 and the bank gave me just under 80%, and they let me amortize it for 30 years, so the payment was low. I got another check when I closed this deal for about $13,000.

Let's take a look at the numbers for house #3.

The Numbers (Purchase)	
ARV	$62,500 (appraised value)
Purchase Price	$28,000
Hard money loan	$35,000 (6 month term)
Initial investment	$0 (the Mortgage was > Purchase Price)
Cash at Close	$ 7,000 (Loan - Purchase Price)
Less Repair Costs	$ 7,000
Cash in Pocket	$ 0 (Cash at Close - Repair Costs)

The Numbers (Refinance)	
Mortgage	$50,000 (refinanced with bank)
Hard money payoff	$35,000 (initial loan)
Hard money interest	$ 2,100 ($350 x 6 months)
Cash in Pocket	$12,900 (Mortgage - Hard money costs)

The Numbers (Rental)	
Monthly Rent	$700
Mortgage	$245
Insurance	$ 65
Taxes	$100
Maintenance	$ 50
Total Expenses	$460
Monthly Cash flow	$240 (Rent - Total Expenses)
Annual Cash flow	$2,880

Houses #4 and #5

For financing on houses #4 & #5, I went through a local bank and had to put 25% down. The loan was for $72,000, so I had to put $18,000 down. Now you see why I was getting cash out at the front end for some of the other deals. As I said, these houses already had long term tenants, but the rents were low.

Let's take a look at the numbers for houses #4 & #5.

The Numbers (Purchase)	
Purchase Price	$72,000 (ARV)
Down Payment	$18,000 (25% of Purchase Price)
Mortgage	$54,000

The Numbers (Rental)	
Monthly Rent	$900 ($450 each)
Mortgage	$356
Insurance	$124
Taxes	$100
Maintenance	$100
Total Expenses	$680
Monthly Cash flow	$220 ($110 each)
Annual Cash flow	$2,640

These tenants eventually left and I was able to charge $650 rent for each house over time, thus increasing my cash flow by $400 a month.

At this point, we had five rental houses, and the combined monthly cash flow was $780. That was $9,360 annually. When you have five investment properties, it will get tougher to do maintenance yourself and hiring a maintenance person becomes very important. Remember, I was still working full time and hiring a maintenance person helped to take some of the burden off of me.

As I mentioned before, the last four houses were purchased in a matter of three days. It was one of the craziest times in my real estate investment life. I was scared, but it was getting easier, and I didn't let the fear stop me.

Conclusion

Don't let fear stop you. Growth is important and necessary if you want to retire, but as you grow, you will have to rely more and more on other people. It is important to build a team of people from various industries to help you execute your dream. I will have a chapter about building a team later in this book. For now, just know that you can't do it all by yourself.

Taxes and Asset Protection

Disclaimer

I am NOT an accountant or a lawyer, so be sure to talk to one before you pursue any of the concepts found in this chapter!

Okay, let's talk about taxes. There are a couple of things that you should know when you are buying and selling properties. If you buy a property and sell it within 12 months of when you purchased it, you will pay capital gains based on the *short term capital gains tax rate*, which generally is your normal tax bracket rate. If you sell the property after 12 months of ownership, then you'll pay the *long term capital gains tax rate* which is 15% to 20% generally. These rates and rules change all the time, so this is a good time to talk about accountants.

Find a good accountant! You want to find one that either invests in real estate themselves or has many clients that are investors. A good accountant can save you a lot of money. My accountant gives great advice during tax season, but also throughout the year as I look at various property and business deals. So find a good accountant.

Limited Liability Companies

Another very important thing that you need to do <u>before</u> you start buying properties is to create a company. When you are investing in rental properties, the preferred company type is a multi-person limited liability company (LLC), but consult with your accountant or lawyer first. My wife and I are the only two members of our LLCs. At some point, you might consider having multiple LLCs, because you don't want to have all of your properties within the same company if you are sued. A limited liability company helps to protect you from lawsuits. It protects your personal assets as well, because if someone falls down and hurts themselves at one of your properties and the property is owned by an LLC, they can only go after the assets that are part of that LLC, unless they can find that you are personally liable for the accident. If you have three properties in that LLC, then the most they could go after you for is the value of those three properties. This is another great conversation to have with your accountant and lawyer.

Separate your money

Protect your money as well by having separate bank accounts for each company. You never want to mix money between companies or between your personal accounts. If you need money from one of your companies, write a check from that company to pay yourself. If you don't separate your money, you effectively take away some of the protections that companies provide.

Tax deductions

I want to talk more about expenses as they relate to income taxes. Some of your *personal* expenses like phone, internet, automobile, etc. can be claimed as expenses to help reduce your income tax. I work from home and use the internet all the time for business. My cell phone is primarily used for business as well. So I can reasonably claim a portion of these *personal* expenses as business expenses. Again, you want to consult your accountant to make sure which expenses can be claimed.

It is important to always operate your business on the up and up!

What other things can be expensed? Your accountant is a great source for that list of items, but here are a few things that you can include. Educational expenses like classes, conferences, trade shows, books, DVDs, and CDs can all be expensed, as long as they are relevant to the business that you conduct. Currently, these can be expensed at 100% of their cost. Let's do some math.

Expenses	
Class on real estate investing	$2,000
Books on real estate investing	$ 300
Conference on Rehabbing Houses	$ 500
Hotel cost for conference	$ 450 ($150 x 3 nights)
Plane ticket to conference	$ 500
Food during conference	$ 250 (only a % can be used)
Total Expenses	**$4,000**

In this example, you have $4,000 that can be counted as expenses against your taxable income. The next table shows the difference in tax you pay.

Taxable Income Calculation	
Annual revenue from business	$10,000
Less expenses	$ 4,000 (from above)
Taxable Income	$ 6,000 (revenue - expenses)

Let's assume that you are taxed at the 25% tax rate. The list below will show you that you are going to save 40% by deducting these expenses.

Tax based on $10,000 is $2,500 (expenses not deducted)
Tax based on $6,000 is $1,500 (expenses deducted)

As you can see, you will save $1,000 in taxes by claiming these educational expenses on your business's income tax return. Divide this savings of $1,000 by your original tax due of $2,500 and you see that you saved 40% by taking these expenses. You'll find that the tax laws were written to benefit businesses. The government really DOES want businesses to succeed, because successful businesses hire more people, pay more taxes, and provide necessary products and services to the people.

Insurance

You've worked hard building your rental real estate portfolio. You started down this path so that you could provide income for your family. You don't want an accident taking all of that away. There are a variety of insurance products that will help protect your investment.

- Property Insurance
- Liability Insurance
- Business Liability Umbrella
- Personal Umbrella

You'll want to have enough *property insurance* on each of your properties to pay for them to be rebuilt in case they are damaged by fire or otherwise. I've only briefly discussed insurance as a line item on your *cash flow* worksheets. An insurance agent is another very important member of your team. A good insurance agent will help you find bundling discounts as well as make sure that you are completely protected. Property insurance covers the building and basically anything that is attached to the property. It will also cover personal property like appliances. It is important to know that property insurance DOES NOT cover the cost of any tenant personal property. We always recommend that tenants purchase *rental insurance* to protect their personal property.

Liability insurance protects you from a potential lawsuit. Let's say that a tenant falls down at one of your properties. In a world that is more than happy to file a lawsuit, there is a chance that the tenant blames you, regardless of whose fault it is. Liability insurance helps protect you from losing your property. The amount of insurance that you have depends on your vulnerability.

Sometimes it is more cost effective to have a single *business liability umbrella* policy that covers all of your properties. This can also be used as a second layer of defense.

If you have a lot of properties and therefore a lot of vulnerability, then you might even consider having another layer of protection called a *personal umbrella*.

Trusts and Wills

Insurance is great for protecting you when you're alive, but what happens to your investments when you die? If you want your investment portfolio to be passed on to your family, then the best way to protect it is through a trust. You'll see that asset protection is done by providing layers of protection. The first layer is a legal entity like corporations and LLCs. As I said before, all rental properties should be held in LLCs. Each of these LLCs should be owned by a *Trust*. Then you, as the *trustee* of the trust, have control over the assets in the trust until you die. At that point, the *beneficiary* (your family or whomever you choose) is given control over the assets. You can set up all sorts of rules for how your beneficiaries receive the assets. Through a trust, you can protect your assets from estate taxes.

A *Will* is used to designate specific wishes. By itself, a Will does not protect your assets from estate taxes.

Estate taxes are charged by the government on assets that are owned by a person who dies. That is, unless they are protected by a trust. Estate tax rates are disgustingly high and I consider them about the worst possible thing that a government could do to a person. For Pete's sake, you just died and your family is in mourning and then the government demands that your beneficiaries pay the government tax so that the assets can be transferred to the beneficiary. Having your assets in a trust will protect them from the government's greedy hands.

Conclusion

When buying real estate investment properties, make sure that you meet with your accountant and determine what type of business entity is best for holding your new assets. Protect your money by having separate bank accounts for businesses and personal use. Minimize the amount of income tax you pay by using the tax laws to deduct business expenses. Protect your assets by holding them in a trust and create a will so that your beneficiaries aren't unnecessarily taxed.

One more deal

I've done a lot of deals and I'm not going to go into detail for all of them, but there are a few more that I would like to talk about. This next deal has some really good aspects and some really bad aspects.

House #6

I've been inside some really nasty houses. Some that were so nasty that I couldn't get out of them fast enough. Almost 100 percent of the time these houses were foreclosed on by the bank. I don't know what goes through the mind of an owner of a house or the tenants that are living in the house, but at some point they must decide that they aren't going to clean anymore and maybe it will be fun to break stuff.

All of these houses have a distinct smell. I don't know what causes this smell, but I used to call it the smell of money. I call it this because most potential buyers, who plan to live in the house, can't get past the smell and decide not to buy it. Many investors are the same. I, however, love these smelly houses because they can be bought for pennies on the dollar. Hence, they smell like money.

Anyway, one day I saw this nice sized house for sale in an okay part of town and decided that we needed to check it out. The pictures that I found online weren't great, but for the most part the house looked okay. We walked into the house and oh my gosh the smell! It definitely smelled like money. It was a bank owned foreclosure and there was junk everywhere inside the house. The carpet definitely had animal waste on it and it was dirty. It was tough to stay inside, but once we plugged our noses and looked passed the dirt, we found that it really was in pretty good shape. I figured it would need paint, flooring, and a new roof and then it would be good.

I calculated the After Repair Value (ARV) at close to be $90,000 and my realtor agreed. The bank was asking $30,000 and I guessed that we would need about $20,000 in repairs. It was looking like it would be a $50,000 investment. The only problem with the $90,000 ARV that I calculated was that the next door neighbor's house looked like a piece of junk. So immediate I took $10,000 off the value and gave it an ARV of $80,000.

You really need to consider the neighborhood when determining the value of a property.

If I was to flip this house, I would make about $22,000 after closing costs. By the way, *flip* means to buy, fix up, and sell. I really liked the house, but I already had a few other projects going on. I decided to come in low and offered $16,000 for the house. My realtor friend laughed at me and never thought that the bank would take the offer, but he presented it regardless. A few days later he was ecstatic. He could not believe that they accepted my offer of $16,000. From that point on, he called me Mr. $16,000 and never laughed at me again when I came in low.

So we bought this house for $16,000 and we did all the work, with the exception of the roof. The neighbors were happy that we were fixing up the house, and some suggested that we buy the other ugly house next door. I did eventually look at that other ugly house. It was a duplex, but it was in real bad shape. I believe my realtor friend ended up buying it a few years later, in a package deal.

The reason that I wanted to talk about this house was twofold. One, because of the amazing price and two, because of a tenant problem that we had with it after we fixed it up. But first let's talk about the purchase of this property.

Let's take a look at the numbers for house #6.

The Numbers (Purchase)	
ARV	$80,000
Purchase Price	$16,000
Repairs	$20,000
Total Investment	$36,000
Down Payment	$ 9,000 (25% of Total Investment)
Mortgage	$27,000

If I were to sell the house, it looked to be a pretty good flip. Here are the potential sales numbers.

The Numbers (Selling as Flipper)	
Sale Price (ARV)	$80,000
Less Closing Costs	$ 8,000 (approximately 10% of Sale Price)
Less Total Cost	$36,000 (from above - Total Investment)
Profit (Cash at Close)	$36,000 (Sale Price - all Costs)

The Cash on Cash Return was a fantastic 400% return!

Profit ÷ Initial Investment = Cash on Cash Return
$36,000 ÷ $9,000 = 400% COCR

However, after trying to sell it ourselves for several months with no success, we decided to advertise it as a *Lease with the Option to Buy*. This is similar to a rent to own, but slightly different.

Lease with the Option to Buy

A lease with the Option to Buy (or Lease Option) is an interesting way to sell a house. There are two pieces to a lease option.

- Option to Buy contract
- Lease (normal rental agreement)

The *Option to Buy* gives a *tenant-buyer* the exclusive right to buy the property from the seller within the term of the lease. To buy this option a tenant-buyer must provide what is called *Option Consideration Money* (OCM) to the seller.

OCM is a <u>non-refundable</u> amount of money that is paid to the seller. If the tenant-buyer fails to complete the sale by the end of the term, they forfeit the OCM. This amount can be whatever you decide.

term is the number of months that the tenant-buyer leases/rents the property. They have to complete the purchase within this term. This time frame can be whatever you decide. I generally do a two year lease option term.

Sale Price is the amount that the property will be sold for by the end of the lease option term. You can increase the sale price to take into account

Clifford T. Wellman Jr.

potential appreciation of the property, if applicable with your housing market.

Inside the Option to Buy contract, you'll include an amount of additional money that a tenant-buyer might earn each month for paying their rent on time. I called this *Earned OCM*. This amount can be whatever you decide.

If the tenant-buyer completes the sale of the property before the end of the term, then all of the Option Consideration Money (including what they earned each month) is applied to the purchase price. This can be considered their down payment. Most lending institutions will recognize this type of down payment.

Additionally, since the house is actually being sold in the future, the seller has the option to appreciate the value of the house, by a percentage each year of the lease. This sale price is included as part of the Option to Buy contract.

In the case of house #6, we asked for a $3,000 OCM and $800 rent per month. If the tenant-buyer were to complete the purchase by the end of the term, then the $3,000 would be applied to the purchase price. An additional $100 out of the monthly rent would also be applied to the purchase price as Earned OCM. So by the time they completed the sale, they would already have paid $5,400 toward the home.

The Lease Option (L/O) Numbers	
ARV	$80,000
L/O Sale Price	$88,200 (based on 5% appreciation / year)
OCM	$ 3,000 (paid to seller by tenant-buyer)
Rent	$ 800
Earned OCM	$ 100 (earned by tenant-buyer monthly)
L/O Term	24 months
Earned OCM Cap	$ 2,400 ($100 x 24 months)
L/O Term OCM	$ 5,400 ($3,000 + $2,400)
Due Seller (Gross)	$82,800 (Sale Price - OCM)
Less Closing Costs	$ 8,820 (10% of L/O Sale Price)
Less Mortgage	$27,000
Less Initial Investment	$ 9,000 (from purchase worksheet above)
Profit	$37,980

How I Retired By Age 45

When you look at these numbers, you might think that the deal isn't that much better then selling it as a flip, which was $36,000 (see *Selling as Flipper* above). However, you need to understand the distinction between *Cash at Close* and *Profit*. In a Lease Option, the profit number needs to include the original OCM that the tenant-buyer paid you at the beginning of the Lease Option term. In this case, $3,000. So now our profit is $40,980. Let's calculate Cash on Cash Return (COCR).

Profit ÷ initial investment = COCR
$40,980 ÷ $9,000 = 455%

Now that looks a little better. Both the initial flip deal and the lease option deal look pretty good. But what needs to be added to the lease option deal is the income earned during the two year lease term. So next we'll calculate the monthly cash flow.

The L/O Numbers	
Rent	$800
Mortgage	$178
Insurance	$100
Taxes	$120
Maintenance	$ 25 (once fixed up and rented)
Total Expenses	$423
Less Earn OCM	$100
Cash flow	$277 (Rent - Total Exp. - Earned OCM)
Annual Cash flow	$3,324
2 Yr L/O Cash flow	$6,648

In addition to the profit of $40,980 that we received when we sold the property, we need to add the cash flow of $6,648 to the profit to determine the true cash on cash return.

True L/O profit $47,628 ($40,980 + $6,648)

Cash on cash return   529% (True L/O profit ÷ Initial Investment)

As you can tell from the numbers, any way you slice it, this is a good deal. There are a few reasons why you might want to sell on a lease option. *First*, it allows you to get some cash up front. *Second*, it allows you to *sell* the property, but avoid paying short term capital gains tax. You avoid short term capital gains tax because the sale date is more than twelve months after the property was purchased. In this case, at least 24 months later after the property was fixed up. *Third*, you collect rent, thus cash flow, during the term of the lease. *Fourth*, you set the sales price at an appreciated value, based on two years into the future. *Fifth*, if the tenant-buyer doesn't complete the sale by the end of the term, they forfeit their option money. *Sixth*, since the tenant is actually renting from you, you continue to hold title to the home. If they quit paying, you simply evict them and you don't have to foreclose on them like you would if you sold it to them on a land contract.

One of the main reasons a tenant-buyer would want a lease option is because they have bad credit and can't get a conventional loan. A lease option gives them two years to fix their credit, so they can get a loan at the end of the lease. I always offer to help a tenant-buyer learn how to improve their credit. Another reason might be that they don't have the necessary down payment required by a bank.

But something went wrong

In this case something went wrong. These tenants ended up being the worst possible tenants we could have dealt with. At some point they stopped paying rent. They gave us excuse after excuse and since we were still new to the real estate investment game, we gave them a break. Up until this point, we had not had any tenant problems, so we really didn't know how to handle it. Each month they would say they were going to get caught up and we would believe them. That was mistake #1. In our defense, they would get caught up, but then they would get behind again. In my opinion, they were professional liars. Eventually we evicted them and they owed us four months back rent. I think the total amount was something like $3,000. We took them to court and received a judgment for $3,000 and shortly after, we began garnishing their wages. However, at some point they decided to declare bankruptcy and as a result we were never able to collect from them. The only good thing about this entire deal was the tenant didn't ruin the house. I'm sure karma will catch up to them at some point.

What lesson did we learn with this lease option deal? If a tenant is late on day one, send them a Demand for Possession letter. This is a form that Michigan requires as the first step in the eviction process. This process might be different in other states, so make sure that you understand the landlord/tenant laws before you get into the real estate investment game. Anyway, the Demand for Possession letter says that the tenant has seven days to either pay or vacate the property. This normally is all a tenant needs to either pay the rent or leave. Even if someone says they will pay the rent in three days, send them the Demand for Possession anyway. If they pay you within three days, great, everything is good. But if they don't pay within three days, then you've wasted three days waiting for them to pay. Every day counts. It might seem heartless, but most people who get into these types of situations have been doing it with every landlord that they've had. Not all of them, but most of them.

Conclusion

A lease option can be a great way to maximize your profit and decrease your tax liability. Also take a firm stand on all tenants when they are late with the rent. Start the eviction process on the day they are late, regardless of when they tell you that they will be paying the rent.

Afterward

We bought and sold several other properties. We also bought several more and held them as rentals. I always tell people who are thinking about investing in rental real estate that they need to buy at least *ten* properties before it starts to get easier. The reason it gets easier after ten is because one or two vacancies won't hurt you financially like they do when you only have three or four properties. Also, when you have ten homes, you will discover that you won't be doing all the work yourself anymore. To get to that point (10 properties), you will have had to build a team around you to do maintenance, accounting, bookkeeping, handle legal issues, etc.

After you reach ten properties, you should begin to realize that your growth rate will accelerate. Now it's time to start buying in bulk.

Go big or go home!

I mentioned in a previous chapter that I used a hard money lender to buy a single family house. The hard money lender and I did a couple deals together and soon started building a good relationship. Up until this point the deals that I did with him were small; less than $50,000 each. It was time to take the next step.

One day I was out to lunch with my realtor friend. We were at our favorite Mexican restaurant, Taco Bell. I lived in a small town and we didn't have a lot of restaurant options. Anyway, I had just been to a class on mobile homes. The cool thing about mobile homes is that you can buy a 3 bedroom mobile home for half the price of a *stick built* home. Stick built is the term used for a house that is built from scratch and not manufactured, like a mobile home. You can buy a mobile home for half the price of a stick built home, but you can get the same amount of rent. Our teacher in the mobile home class said that mobile homes are like little boxes that spit out money, and he was right. Let's look at some numbers:

I had been buying houses for about $40,000 (after repairs). Some for more. Some for less. I was finding similarly sized mobile homes for $20,000. I could rent both homes for the same amount. In our small town, the going rent for a 3 bedroom home was between $650 and $750, so let's use $700 for our purposes. Already you should be able to see the benefit of buying mobile homes over stick built homes.

Purchase	Stick Built	Mobile Home
Investment	$40,000	$20,000
Down Payment	$ 8,000	$ 4,000
Mortgage Amount	$32,000	$16,000

You can already see that the investment amount is less when buying a mobile home. Next we'll look at the cash flow numbers.

How I Retired By Age 45

Rent Numbers	Stick Built	Mobile Home
Monthly Rent	$700	$700
Mortgage	$211	$105
Insurance	$ 75	$ 50
Taxes	$100	$100
Maintenance	$ 50	$ 50
Total Expenses	$436	$305
Monthly Cash flow	$264	$395
Annual Cash flow	$3,168	$4,740
Annual Return *	39.6%	118.5%

* cash on cash return

Both deals look good, but the mobile home deal is FAR better. Next, consider that I had $8,000 to spend in total. If I buy two mobile homes instead of a single stick built home, I would be earning $790 in monthly cash flow, which is about three times the income of a single stick built home.

Mobile homes were really intriguing to me and this was just the beginning. I had begun looking at mobile home parks online and decided that it was time to start visiting a few. So back to lunch at Taco Bell.

I was eating a chili cheese burrito and I mentioned to my realtor friend that I was interested in buying a mobile home park and he loved the idea. At the time, he had just purchased a few apartment complexes in our town and had tripled the number of units that he owned. He was excited that I was kind of doing the same thing as him. Within the week we started looking at mobile home parks. I personally visited at least 20 mobile home parks before I finally was ready to put in an offer on one. I had looked at over 100 mobile home parks online.

I want to back up a moment, because I need to talk about something that is very important.

"Money?" you ask.

Yes, where was I going to get the money to buy an entire mobile home park? I had done pretty good so far and had a nice bit of cash flow coming in each

Clifford T. Wellman Jr.

month, but I still didn't have the necessary cash to buy an entire mobile home park. The park that I was looking at was going to cost me $665,000! At the time, that amount of money was crazy! Remember fear? I was really scared at this point.

I had talked to a few banks and several weren't interested. It was too much money, and many of them had held loans on mobile home parks in the past that had gone bad. I knew that buying a mobile home park was a good deal, so I had to figure out how to make the deal happen. The park had 76 lots, but only had 28 homes. So there was tremendous growth potential. The park was newer, less than 20 years old, so the infrastructure was good. When you start looking at multiunit properties like mobile home parks and apartment complexes, you have to start worrying about roads, sewer, water, lights, etc. It's not just a house you're buying, you're buying an entire community. Some mobile home parks actually have mini sewer treatment plants. This park was on municipal sewer, so I didn't have to worry about that. It did have a couple wells, so I had to deal with all the state regulations for providing water to customers.

Let's get back to the money. Since I was having trouble with banks, I decided to go to my hard money guy. I was in the habit of asking him about various types of businesses that he had invested in, so I asked him if he ever owned a mobile home park. That got us talking. Anyway, to make a long story short, he ended up asking me if I needed money for the park. I said that I did and he asked how much. I told him and he said to write up a plan and he'd be ready to lend me the money. I was ecstatic.

I spent the next couple days finalizing the plan that I already started and within a week we agreed to the terms. So now talk about being scared. Do you remember when I said that I paid him 12% interest on previous loans? Well, that turns out to be a 1% payment each month. On a $665,000 loan, I would be paying him $6,650 in interest each month. Oh! I forgot to tell you that it was an interest only loan! In this case, I would be paying him his interest each month, for up to 18 months. So going from a $50,000 deal for a single family home to $665,000 for a mobile home park was really crazy. However, I learned something really important while working on this deal. It takes almost the same amount of work to do the $50,000 deal as it does the

$665,000 deal. So why would I ever waste my time buying a single family home ever again? The other thing about a deal like this is that all the numbers are bigger. You might as well just add a zero at the end of everything; revenue, expenses, taxes, insurance, etc.

Normally, when you buy a small single family home, the seller asks you to provide what is called a good faith deposit. This shows the seller that you are serious. In Michigan, this money is held in an escrow account with the realtor or with a lawyer. Usually, on a single family home, I would put down $500 to $1,000 depending on the deal. With a bigger deal like this mobile home park, I would have to put down something larger. Some sellers wanted anywhere from $10,000 to $50,000 on a deal this size. I was in growth mode and I was spending money like crazy to keep growing, so needless to say, I didn't have that much money to put down. As a matter of fact, all I had was $3,500. When we put my offer in with the $3,500 good faith deposit, the seller ended up calling me Mr. $3,500. It was funny actually, but he accepted the offer. The guy was a little bit eccentric. I'm trying to be nice here. Simply put, it was difficult dealing with this guy, but in the end it was worth it.

My original investment on the $665,000 deal was $3,500! I still laugh about that. It even gets better, because when I finally closed on the sale, I got my original $3,500 good faith deposit back. I had asked my hard money lender for the entire $665,000, so the $3,500 that I had already put down, I got back at close. So, as it turns out, my original investment was actually zero. Yep, I bought a mobile home park with no money down! This was in January of 2012.

Time to build it up

As you already know, the park had 28 homes in it, ten of which I bought as part of the deal. Even though I was paying $6,650 per month in interest payments, the park was still generating cash flow. However, there wasn't quite enough cash flow for me to retire yet. I needed to get more homes into the park. You might recall that I said earlier I could spend $20,000 on a mobile home. This price actually included having the mobile home moved into the park and completely set up. I was collecting $300 for lot rent for each home in the park. I was collecting an additional $400 for home rent, for each

Clifford T. Wellman Jr.

of the homes that I owned. So for each home in the park, I was collecting $3,600 in lot rent each year. Remember that is just lot rent. We haven't talked about home rent yet.

It's time to talk about how the value of a mobile home park is calculated. The value is based on the Net Operating Income (NOI). NOI is calculated by subtracting expenses from revenue (just like we did for passive income). By the way, your mortgage is not included in expenses when calculating NOI.

Revenue - Expenses = Net Operating Income (NOI)

From this formula we can also infer the following two formulas:

Revenue - NOI = Expenses
Expenses + NOI = Revenue

To determine the value of the property, you divide the NOI by a Capitalization Rate (or cap rate), which is a percentage. Mobile home parks generally use a 10% cap rate. If the park is in fantastic condition, you could go as high as 8%, and as low as 14%, if it is a dump. I have always used 10% for my park because it is a pretty typical park. It is in good shape and has nice houses in it, but it isn't full and doesn't have some amenities that some really nice parks have.

Based on the information that I've already provided, you should be able to tell me what the NOI for this park was. Let me give you a hint:

NOI ÷ cap rate = Value

We already know the *value* was $665,000 and the cap rate was 10%, so we can solve this formula for NOI (let's crack open your algebra book). Just kidding, I'm not going to make you crack open an algebra book.

Value x cap rate = NOI
$665,000 x 0.10 = $66,500

So we calculated the NOI to be $66,500 based on the purchase price of $665,000 and using a cap rate of 10% (0.10).

Another interesting bit of information is that most mobile home parks, that are managed well, have an expense ratio of 40%. This means that expenses equal 40% of revenue. For example, if you have $100,000 in revenue, then your expenses should be about $40,000, and your resulting NOI should be $60,000. Based on that, we can calculate what the *Revenue* and *Expenses* should be for the park that I was about to purchase.

If you enjoy math, here is a fun little exercise:

Revenue x 40% = Expenses

If you apply this formula above to the NOI formula of:

Revenue - Expenses = NOI

We get:

Revenue - (Revenue x 40%) = NOI

Do you see how I replaced *Expenses* with *(Revenue x 40%)*? This formula reduces to:

Revenue x 60% = NOI   **OR**
NOI ÷ 60% = Revenue

So if we insert our NOI of $66,550 we get:

NOI ÷ 60% = Revenue
$66,500 ÷ .60 = $110,883

This tells us that the projected Revenue should be $110,883 for the park if it is managed properly. Using the formula above we can calculate the expected Expenses:

Revenue - NOI = Expense
$110,883 - $66,500 = $44,383

Now that we've calculated all of the expected Revenue and Expense numbers based on the estimated NOI, we should have an idea where we stand financially.

Clifford T. Wellman Jr.

So with all of the information that I just provided, you should be able calculate the following for my park when I bought it.

Revenues	$108,333 (calculated)
Expenses	$ 44,333 (calculated)
NOI	$ 66,500 (estimated)
Value (calculated)	$665,000 (NOI ÷ cap rate of 10%)

Now that you see the relationship between Value, NOI, Revenue, and Expenses, we can use some of these formulas to estimate the value of a property.

As part of my due diligence, I requested actual Revenue and Expense numbers from the seller. By the way, if a seller won't provide these numbers, walk away! The seller provided three years of detailed financials, so I had a lot of data to crunch. Here are the basics:

Interestingly, the real numbers looked more like this:

Revenues	$145,000 (actual)
Expenses	$ 57,000 (actual)
NOI	$ 88,000 (calculated)
Value (calculated)	$880,000 (NOI ÷ cap rate of 10%)

Based on these numbers, I was about to buy a property worth $880,000 for $665,000! That is an instant $215,000 in equity (net worth). Remember my initial investment of $0. I made $215,000 out of nothing, just by buying this park. Let's look at the expense ratios as well. If we divide *Expense* by *Revenues* we get a percentage of 39.3%, so that puts this park in line with the 40% ratio that I mentioned earlier.

A little reminder about NOI, it doesn't include your debt service (your loan payments). That is why determining NOI is so important. It will tell you immediately if you can afford to purchase a property based on the calculated value. If you know the NOI and if you have a mortgage calculator, you can determine within seconds what amount of cash flow you can expect to collect each month. Let's do a little more math!

You might recall that I was going to pay my hard money lender $6,650 each month in interest. That puts my annual debt service at $79,800!

Annual NOI	$88,000
Annual Loan Interest	$79,800 ($6,650 x 12)
Annual Cashflow	$ 8,200
Monthly Cashflow	$ 683 (rounded to nearest dollar)

This new purchase was going to immediately generate $683 in monthly passive income. That isn't that great for such a big deal, but that is primarily because of my high interest rate. If I were to refinance the property at 5% interest, my new loan payment would be $4,388 based on 5% interest at a 20 year amortization. This is a reduction of $2,262 in my monthly loan payment. All of that goes to the bottom line cash flow number. However, virtually no commercial lender would allow me to refinance a loan this size without first seeing the property perform for 12-18 months. So I would have to wait a while before I would be able to reap the benefits of a refinanced mortgage.

Regardless, I got a great deal on the mobile home park, but adding only $683 a month in passive income didn't push me over the edge and allow me to retire. It was time to get to work. First, I needed to add homes to the park and second, I needed to work on getting the park refinanced with a bank to reduce the amount of interest that I was paying. Both of these tasks would increase my cash flow, hopefully to the point where I could retire.

This was the starting point when I bought the park. If you look at a mobile home park and find that the expense ratio is a lot lower than 40%, then it is possible that the seller isn't including everything in his list of expenses. If the ratio is a lot higher, then maybe the park is poorly managed. Forty percent is just a good base line. Do your due diligence and make sure you understand what is going on with the property that you are purchasing.

Adding mobile homes to the park

When you add a mobile home to the park, there generally is very little additional monthly expenses. Earlier in this chapter, I said that the NOI for each mobile home was $3,600. I'm going to reduce that number to $3,250 to account for potential vacancies. This calculates to about 10% vacancy rate. Ten percent is a conservative number for my mobile home park, but it is better to be conservative when trying to calculate these numbers. So we are using $3,250 as the annual NOI for each mobile home that I add to the park, and if I divide the NOI of the mobile home by the 10% cap rate, I come up with a value of $32,500. This is $32,500 for lot rent alone. So when I added a $20,000 home to the park I was increasing the value of the park by $52,500 ($20,000 + $32,500)! That is a 262.5% return on investment!

The Numbers (Mobile Homes)	
Mobile Home Price	$20,000
Monthly Lot Rent	$ 300
Annual Lot Rent (NOI)	$ 3,250 (reduced by 10% for vacancy)
Value Added for Rent	$32,500 (NOI ÷ cap rate of 10%)
Total Value	$52,500 ($32,500 + $20,000)
Initial Investment	$20,000
Cash on cash return	262.5% (Total Value ÷ Initial Investment)

How could I go wrong with the 262.5% return on my investment? Anyway, I went out and got money for six new mobile homes. I spent $120,000 and increased the value of the park by $315,000. In twelve months, I had increased the value of my mobile home park to more than a million dollars. A few months later, I refinanced the mobile home park and reduced my loan payment to $5,200 and pulled out some more cash to buy even more mobile homes. Here is a look at the numbers after twelve months.

Revenues	$ 180,000
Expenses	$ 60,000
NOI	$ 120,000
Value (calculated)	$1,200,000 (NOI ÷ cap rate of 10%)

This is what my new cash flow situation looked like:

Annual NOI	$120,000
Annual Loan Interest	$ 62,400 ($5,200 x 12)
Annual Cashflow	$ 57,600
Monthly Cashflow	$ 4,800

In twelve months, my *monthly cash flow* on the mobile home park jumped from $683 to $4,800. Add that to my other real estate investment cash flow and it was time for me to retire. Actually, I saw the writing on the wall prior to refinancing the mobile home park and in October of 2012 (six weeks before my 45th birthday), I got out of the software development industry. I went from zero cash flow to retirement in five short years! Imagine if I had started this when I was 25!

Anyway, five years after I purchased the mobile home park, there were 58 homes in the park and it was valued at about $2.3 million dollars. My initial investment of $3,500, oh wait, I mean $0, had turned into a $2.3 million property.

Conclusion

It takes almost the same amount of work to put together a $50,000 deal as it does to put together a $665,000 deal. For the most part, you can simply add a zero to all the numbers within the calculations. Buying in bulk is the fastest way to retirement, but you have to start small. Buy one property and then another until you have ten properties or so. Then, with some cash in the bank and with some cash flow, start looking at multi-unit properties like mobile home parks and apartment complexes. Make sure you build your team along the way. Establish relationships with realtors, bankers, bookkeepers, accountants, lawyers, insurance agents, and maintenance personnel. Once you get to this point, your job should be 100% management. You shouldn't be doing maintenance or bookkeeping, your job is to find the next deal. It's also time to find a property manager.

Let's make a plan

In the previous chapters, I talked about some of the possibilities that are out there. Hopefully, most of my examples gave you a little motivation to create a retirement plan for yourself. In this chapter, I want to walk you through the goal setting and planning process. Achieving your dreams will take work, but once you get there, you'll be happy that you spent time and did the work.

Turn your dream into a goal

Okay, now it's time for you to define your goal. Write it down on a 8.5" x 11" piece of paper. I don't care if you do this on a computer or with a pen, just write it down now.

RETIRE BY THE AGE 45

Write it in big letters, so that you can see it clearly from across the room. By the way, you don't have to limit yourself to one goal. You are more than capable of achieving many goals, but be careful not to spread yourself too thin. Maybe for now just write down one long term goal like the one that I wrote down above and then write down another smaller goal that will be a stepping stone toward your big goal.

BUY A JET SKI

That was one of my short term goals. It's a fun goal to aim for while you build up your business. Maybe you're like me and just can't wait until the end to have some fun. But DONT LET A SMALL GOAL GET IN THE WAY OF THE MAIN GOAL! Sorry I had to yell at you, but it is important not to lose focus on the end game.

Let's make a plan

First we'll make a plan for achieving our primary goal, in my case Retiring By Age 45. Obviously, your goal will be different, but all the same steps apply. To achieve our goal of retiring by age 45, we really need to understand what that means. We need to identify all of the metrics that we'll use to determine if we've actually achieved the goal. For instance, the main metric for determining if we can retire is the comparison of income to expenses. We know that income must be greater than expenses, but we need a concrete number to aim for. Understand that this number (amount of expenses) is always changing, but we have to start somewhere. So go back to the exercise we did on listing expenses and put that number down.

Expenses are equal to $4,000 per month.

I've selected $4,000 as the amount of expenses that I will have when I retire. Next, let's give ourselves a time frame. Let's assume you're 35 and you want to retire by the time you are 45, that means you have 10 years to achieve this goal.

10 year time frame.

Ten years is a long time. A lot can happen during ten years. This is why we need to set other short term goals, and we need to periodically examine where we are against the plan, and then change the plan as necessary.

So, now we know that we need at least $4,000 in monthly passive income and we need to achieve this amount within a ten year period. So let's look at what it takes to achieve $4,000 in monthly passive income. In my examples earlier in this book, there was a range of cash flow associated with each property. For simplicity, let's use $200 cash flow (monthly passive income) per unit (single family home). If each unit earns $200 a month in cash flow, then we know that we need to own 20 units to achieve $4,000 in monthly cash flow.

20 units need to be purchased within the 10 year time frame.

This gives us more detail on what we need to do to reach our goal. One side note that I would like to discuss, is the idea of vacancy. Regardless of how awesome your properties are, you'll have properties go vacant on occasion. It is important that you consider some vacancy percentage in all of your cash flow estimates. I include vacancy rate as an expense in each of the individual units, so that the final cash flow number reflects a vacancy percentage. The actual percentage depends on your market, and the type of unit that you are dealing with. Single family homes will have different vacancy rates than

Clifford T. Wellman Jr.

apartments, which will have different rates than mobile home parks. Ask your realtor what the vacancy rates are in the market that you are in. Also use demographic data from websites like www.city-data.com to get these numbers. For our example, assume that the $200 average cash flow number has already taken into account some vacancy rate. Five to ten percent is probably a good starting point.

Okay, so we have to buy 20 units in 10 years. That is equal to 2 units per year or 1 unit every 6 months. One unit every six months is very attainable.

Buy 2 units per year for ten years.

By now you should see that we are drilling down into your original goal and see that buying 20 units really isn't that hard, knowing that you have to buy 1 unit every six months.

Obviously all these numbers are totally dependent on the type of property that you are investing in. In my market, I am buying houses that have an ARV (After Repair Value) of between $50,000 and $80,000. As a rule of thumb, I always buy a house at a discount of 70-80% of the ARV. So if we are buying a house that has an ARV of $50,000, then my total investment is going to be between $35,000 and $40,000. Remember total investment includes the purchase price, repair costs, and holding costs.

"Holding costs? What are those?" you ask.

Right! We haven't talked about holding costs yet. When you buy an investment property you almost always have to do some work to it. You can assume that you'll own the property for 3-6 months before you are able to rent it out. Or maybe the rental market is slow and you have difficulty renting it. Anyway, *holding costs* are the amount of money that you'll spend on the property each month while you fix it up. This doesn't include any of the repairs or maintenance. *Holding costs* include expenses like mortgage, taxes, insurance, utilities, etc. There might be other costs, but these are the primary expenses. Just sit down and think of all the expenses that you'll have while you wait for the repairs and maintenance to be completed. Again, the cost of repairs and maintenance is NOT included in *holding costs*.

Holding Costs Example	
Mortgage	$200
Insurance	$100
Taxes	$100
Gas Utilities	$ 50
Electric Utilities	$ 50
Water/Sewer Utility	$ 50
Total Holding Costs	**$550 (per month)**

If you are planning to work on the property for three months, you might want to include six months in holding costs, just to account for overruns of the project to perform repairs on the home. So, in our example, you'll need to include $3,300 ($550 x 6 months) in holding costs as part of your ARV calculation. Okay, back to the plan.

Now we know that we have to buy one rental property every six months to meet our goal. I recommend that you revisit your plan and compare it to your actual progress, at least once a year. I like to do this at the end of the year as I'm preparing a *Profit and Loss Statement (P&L)* for each business. I send each P&L to my accountant so that he can prepare my tax returns. At the same time I update my *Personal Financial Statement (PFS)* as well. For now just understand that both of these documents will show you how you are doing financially. Banks will require a PFS whenever you ask them for money. So it's a good idea to get familiar with that document.

So far we have the following metrics and action items on our plan:

Goal: Retire by the age 45
Timeframe: 10 years
Primary Metric: Earn at least $4,000 in monthly passive income
Primary Action Item: Buy 20 rental units within 10 years
Sub Action Item: Buy 1 rental unit every 6 months

Now we have a plan and action items to achieve our goal. The next chapter will go into detail for achieving the first action item, which is to buy one rental unit.

How to find your first property

In this chapter, I will give you step by step instructions for buying your first single family home rental. Based on our plan, we need to purchase a rental property that will add $200 in monthly cash flow. To start, I am going to focus on buying a single family home. So let's get started. Here is a basic outline of the steps.

Step 1: Determine what type of property to buy

Step 2: Get pre-approved for a loan

Step 3: Find a property

Step 4: Visit the property

Step 5: Put an offer on the property

Step 6: Close on the property

Step 7: Perform repairs on the property

Step 8: Rent the property

Step 9: Manage the property

Step 1: Determine what type of property to buy

When you look at the city that you live in, you know that there are a variety of different neighborhoods to choose from. These neighborhoods vary by house prices, rental rates, crime rates, and other demographics. For simplicity, I want to identify five different types of neighborhoods.

1. Very high priced neighborhoods
2. High priced neighborhoods
3. Medium priced neighborhoods
4. Lower priced neighborhoods
5. Very low priced neighborhoods.

Regardless of where you are in the United States, each city will have these types of neighborhoods. Just remember that houses in a #1 neighborhood of a small town will be priced drastically different from houses in a #1 neighborhood of large metropolitan areas. This is true of all five neighborhood types. Fortunately, the rental rates should follow a similar curve as the property values.

Okay, I would argue that we want to avoid the #1 and #5 neighborhoods. The houses in the #1 neighborhoods will be far too expensive and will be difficult to rent. If you want to focus on these types of neighborhoods that is fine, just know that your tenant pool is very small, so renting may be difficult. As for #5 neighborhoods, these properties will generally be in bad condition and may require extensive repairs. This is my primary reason for avoiding #5 neighborhoods. Additionally, #5 neighborhoods generally have higher crime rates and the type of tenant that you will attract will generally be those who have very low income or are on some sort of government assistance. My experience with tenants who are on government assistance is not good. In my experience they are less likely to take good care of your property. I always want to find tenants who will take good care of my properties. You can find good tenants in #5 neighborhoods, but it can be difficult.

Let's talk about the other three neighborhood types. My favorites are #3 and #4, because I can usually get great values in these neighborhoods, but it is all up to you. #2 neighborhoods can be good if you have enough tenants who are willing to pay higher end rental rates. Let's break each neighborhood down.

Neighborhood #2

- properties will cost more
- if you are buying the property with a conventional mortgage, then you'll have to come to the table with more money. Most banks (and credit unions) want 20-25% down
- the number of repairs could be less than neighborhoods #3 & #4
- tenants expect higher end fixtures and amenities, so you might end up spending more money on repairs even though you are doing less work
- some of these neighborhoods have association fees, which you'll have to pass on to your tenants, which will require you to have higher rental rates
- rental rates will be higher

Clifford T. Wellman Jr.

- taxes will be higher
- insurance costs will be higher

Let's go through an example neighborhood #2 property. Remember, all these numbers will be different depending on the area where you are buying properties.

The Purchase Numbers (Neighborhood #2)	
ARV	$150,000
Purchase Price	$140,000 (we buy at a discount)
Down Payment	$ 28,000
Mortgage Amount	$112,000
Holding Costs *	$ 8,760 ($1,460 x 6 months)

The Rental Numbers (Neighborhood #2)	
Rent	$1,700
Vacancy	$ 85 (5% of Rent)
Mortgage Payment *	$ 860
Insurance *	$ 150
Taxes *	$ 300
Maintenance	$ 100
Total Expenses	$1,495
Monthly Cash flow	$ 205 (Rent - Total Expenses)
Annual Cash flow	$2,460

* included in Holding Costs ($1,310 total, plus $150 for utilities equals $1,460 total)

The numbers above reflect my best guess at our imaginary neighborhood. The only one that is accurate is the Mortgage Payment number which was calculated using the loan amount and amortizing the loan for 20 years at 6% interest. While I'm thinking about it, I highly recommend that you install a mortgage calculator on your phone so that you can quickly run these numbers. The one that I use is called *Karl's Mortgage Calculator.* It is free in the Google Play Store (and I assume the Apple Store). I use it a lot! Anyway, back to the numbers. You'll have to plug in your own numbers for insurance, taxes, and maintenance, based on your market. Usually, I have an idea what the insurance and taxes are before I actual visit a property. I can almost always calculate what my cash flow should be before I step onto the property. Also, understand that higher end properties have higher end maintenance costs. In this case, my total expenses equaled $1,495, so I chose a nice round number of $1,700 for my rental rate. This gives us $205 in monthly cash flow. Your realtor should be able to help you with the rental rates in your area. There are several websites that provide average rental rates in a given area. I like to use *www.rentometer.com*. You enter an address and a desired rental amount and it will show you where you stand in your market. It will also show you various comparable rentals in your area. Let's say you do all of this analysis and you discover that the market will only bear a rent rate of $1,400. You will know that this house is not the one for you because your monthly expense are greater than the expected rental rate. The only exception might be that you can get the property for a far better price.

Neighborhood #3

- properties will be reasonably priced
- the number of repairs could be more than neighborhood #2
- tenants will expect average fixtures and less amenities, so you could end up spending less money on repairs even though you are doing more work
- no association fees
- medium rental rates
- medium taxes
- medium insurance

Let's go through an example neighborhood #3 property.

The Purchase Numbers (Neighborhood #3)	
ARV	$80,000
Purchase Price	$70,000 (we buy at a discount)
Down Payment	$14,000
Mortgage Amount	$56,000
Holding Costs *	$ 4,800 ($800 x 6 months)

The Rental Numbers (Neighborhood #3)	
Rent	$1,000
Vacancy	$ 50 (5% of Rent)
Mortgage Payment *	$ 400
Insurance *	$ 100
Taxes *	$ 150
Maintenance	$ 75
Total Expenses	$ 775
Monthly Cash flow	$ 225 (Rent - Total Expenses)
Annual Cash flow	$2,700

* included in Holding Costs ($650 total, plus $150 for utilities equals $800 total)

You do all the same analysis prior to seeing this property as you did with the property in neighborhood #2. As a general rule, I look at 10 properties online or on paper before I visit one. I visit 10 properties before I put an offer on one. You may end up putting in multiple offers before actually closing on one. For every offer that you put on a property, you'll have to look at about 100 properties. Don't forget, you can *look* at most of these properties online or on paper. So you see, you'll want to be able to make decisions fast, so that you aren't wasting time. This is a guideline and not a rule.

Neighborhood #4

- properties will be priced lower
- the number of repairs could be more than neighborhoods #2 and #3
- tenants will expect average fixtures and no amenities, so you will end up spending less money on repairs even though you are doing more work
- no association fees
- lower rental rates
- lower taxes
- lower insurance

Let's go through an example neighborhood #4 property.

The Purchase Numbers (Neighborhood #4)	
ARV	$50,000
Purchase Price	$40,000 (we buy at a discount)
Down Payment	$ 8,000
Mortgage Amount	$32,000
Holding Costs *	$ 3,390 ($565 x 6 months)

The Rental Numbers (Neighborhood #4)	
Rent	$750
Vacancy	$ 35 (5% of Rent)
Mortgage Payment *	$230
Insurance *	$ 85
Taxes *	$100
Maintenance	$ 50
Total Expenses	$500
Monthly Cash flow	$250 (Rent - Total Expenses)
Annual Cash flow	$3,000

* included in Holding Costs ($415 total, plus $150 for utilities equals $565 total)

You should notice the trend that I tried to illustrate. This trend is not always perfect, but in my experience it is pretty close. If you didn't notice, the trend is that you earn more cash flow with a smaller investment, when buying homes in neighborhood #4. Let's compare all three.

The Buy Numbers	#2	#3	#4
ARV	$150,000	$80,000	$50,000
Purchase Price	$140,000	$70,000	$40,000
Down Payment	$ 28,000	$14,000	$ 8,000
Loan Amount	$112,000	$56,000	$32,000
Holding Costs *	$ 8,760	$ 4,800	$ 3,390

The Rent Numbers	#2	#3	#4
Rent	$1,700	$1,000	$ 750
Vacancy	$ 85	$ 50	$ 35
Mortgage Payment *	$ 860	$ 400	$ 230
Insurance *	$ 150	$ 100	$ 85
Taxes *	$ 300	$ 150	$ 100
Maintenance	$ 100	$ 75	$ 50
Total Expenses	$1,495	$ 775	$ 500
Monthly Cash flow	$ 205	$ 225	$ 250
Annual Cash flow	$2,460	$2,700	$3,000
COCR	8.875%	19.285%	37.5%

* included in Holding Costs

So you should notice a few things here:

- the better the neighborhood, the more your initial investment will be
- the better the neighborhood, the higher your maintenance costs
- the better the neighborhood, the higher the holding costs
- the better the neighborhood, the higher the taxes
- the better the neighborhood, the higher the insurance
- the better the neighborhood, the higher the mortgage payment
- the lower the neighborhood, the higher your cash flow can be

There are probably more things that we can point out, but the things that I want you to take away from this are:

- If you have $28,000 in cash, you can buy <u>one property</u> in neighborhood #2 and make $2,460 in annual cash flow. That is a 8.785% annual cash on cash return. That is $205 in monthly cash flow toward your goal.
- If you have $28,000 in cash, you can buy <u>two properties</u> in neighborhood #3 and make $5,400 in annual cash flow. That is a 19.285% annual cash on cash return. That is $450 in monthly cash flow toward your goal.

- If you have $24,000 (notice it is less than the other two examples), you can buy <u>three properties</u> in neighborhood #4 and make $9,000 in annual cash flow. That is a 37.5% annual cash on cash return. That is $750 in monthly cash flow toward your goal.

Which of these examples is the best choice?

"But won't I have more problems with tenants in neighborhood #4 than in neighborhoods #2 and #3?" you ask.

The answer to that question is: It all depends on how you interview your potential tenants. You can find bad tenants in every neighborhood. Just because people have less money, doesn't mean they will treat your property badly. It is important to check all job references and rental history references regardless of where the property is located. Always take a security deposit that is equal to at least one month's rent. In Michigan, you can take up to 150% of the rent for a security deposit. So if the rent rate is $1,000, then you can take up to $1,500 for security deposit. No tenant gets to move in without the first month's rent and security deposit. That right there will help you screen out a lot of bad tenants.

Remember that this entire exercise was to help you determine what your price range is and in what neighborhoods your future properties reside.

Step 2: Get pre-approved for a loan

Once you've figured out what type of properties you want to buy, it's time to get pre-approved for a loan. Go visit as many local banks and credit unions as possible and see if they can pre-approve you for a loan. Tell them that you are looking to invest in rental real estate. If they see you as a serious investor, they'll see you as repeat business. If possible, bring them a copy of your credit report and see if they'll verbally pre-approve you before running your credit. Every time a bank or other organization pulls your credit, your credit score is negatively affected. It doesn't hurt your score too much, but some banks won't like to see a lot of activity all at once. There are several free credit check sites that you can use to pull your own credit without the adverse affects. I like to use www.creditkarma.com. So sign up for free by entering

Clifford T. Wellman Jr.

your social security information, probably your birthday and a few other personal details and get a free credit report. I check my credit multiple times a year.

I recommend that you put together a package that contains the following information for the banks or credit unions:

- a recent credit report
- a Personal Financial Statement (PFS)
- be prepared to provide all personal and business tax returns (this can probably be during a follow up visit)
- pay stubs from your job for a couple months
- a list of bank accounts with balances (no account numbers)
- request a certain amount to be pre-approved for

This package will give them virtually everything they need, and it will show them that you are organized and professional. Bankers and accountants love it when they deal with organized people.

NOTE: When the bank or credit union pre-approves you, they should give you a letter stating that you are pre-approved for up to a certain amount.

When you talk to the loan officer, ask them if they'll give you a loan based on the appraised value of the property and not necessarily the actual purchase price. Remember, we want to buy properties at a discount. So a property that will appraise for $50,000, you might only have to pay $30,000 for it. If the bank will give you 80% of the $50,000, then that means they will give you $40,000 total. This will give you $10,000 toward the repairs.

Also ask the loan officer what the minimum down payment percent is, what interest rate you'll be paying, and how many years the loan will be amortized. When you are first starting out, I recommend that you try to get as long of a term as possible on the amortization schedule. Some banks will only give you a 15 year term. Some will give 20, 25, or 30 years. The longer the term, the lower your mortgage payment will be, and conversely the higher your cash flow will be. Once you have more cash and more cash flow, you can start doing shorter amortization lengths and higher down payments to reduce your debt. Almost all commercial loans will include a 5 or 10 year balloon. Let's look at an example.

The Numbers (5 year balloon at 6% amortized over 20 years)	
Purchase Price	$50,000 (including repairs)
Down Payment	$10,000
Loan Amount	$40,000
Mortgage Payment	$286.57
Balloon Payment	$33,959.84

So the bank expects this balloon payment of $33,959.84 to be paid at the end of the 5 year period.

"WAIT! WHAT? I can't pay that!" you exclaim.

I know, I know, but what actually will happen is you'll refinance the entire loan when the balloon payment comes due. The new loan will be based on the new interest rates (five years in the future). This could be good or bad depending on what the rates have been doing for the past five years. But there is also the possibility that the property has appreciated. In five years, your $50,000 property could now be worth $65,000. We are five years into your ten year plan and you're still buying properties, so what if you asked the bank to refinance the loan at $52,000 (which is 80% of the $65,000 newly appraised value). In this case, if you refinance for $52,000, you would pay off the balloon payment and probably some closing costs, and then have around $17,000 in cash to invest in your next property. BUT WAIT! Before you do that, make sure that your property can handle an increased mortgage payment. Hopefully rental rates have also increased during these five years and your cash flow numbers stay the same. If your cash flow numbers are good, then maybe you take out some cash to reinvest. I'll let you get out your mortgage calculator and run your own "what-if" scenarios on the other amortization lengths.

Step 3: Find a property

Now you know in what neighborhood you want to look for properties. You know your maximum price range based on the pre-approval letter from the bank. It's time to talk to your realtor. Set up a meeting and discuss what types of properties you are looking for and give him/her a copy of your pre-approval letter. That way, he can tell the sellers that you are pre-approved to buy their property. This tells the realtor and any sellers that you are serious. Ask the realtor to put you on an automated email system that will send you new listings as they become available. Tell them price range, number of bedrooms, number of baths, size of lot, etc. Whatever your criteria is. For the record, I only buy 3+ bedroom single family homes. In the markets that I am in, these properties rent and sell faster. Two bedroom homes just don't sell fast and don't bring in as much rent. Your market might be different. Don't forget to do your research. Hopefully, your realtor (who is also an investor) will advise you on these things.

Your realtor is busy. He is trying to make a living, too. Most realtors prefer to list homes for sellers, versus work with buyers. However, a good realtor will want to work with a buyer/investor like yourself, because they know that you'll be buying more than one property. They also know that you're not an emotional buyer, and by that I mean that you aren't buying a home to live in. You are buying a property that will make you cash flow. IT IS ALL ABOUT THE NUMBERS! Sorry to yell, but you really need to understand that it is all about the numbers. Anyway, realtors are busy and they do have other customers. So you'll actually have to do some work to find properties. Use the internet to help with your search. www.realtor.com and www.zillow.com are my favorite websites, but there are a lot of other local websites out there. You might consider craigslist, but I don't spend a lot of time there.

Don't just rely on your realtor or the internet. Get out there and drive around. There are a lot of properties that are for sale by owner. These deals can be a little trickier to do, because you are dealing directly with a seller who might be emotional. There are also bank owned foreclosures out there, too. Most foreclosure properties will have some posting on the house (usually the front door) that says the property is being foreclosed. This posting will have the name and contact information of the bank that owns it. Call that bank. If it's summer time, look for a property that has tall grass. In the winter, look for the property that hasn't been plowed or shoveled. Often foreclosures will be unkempt in both the summer and winter. I already told you to call the bank that has the foreclosure posting on the door, but other local banks and credit unions may have properties that have been foreclosed on, or better yet, are in the process of being foreclosed. See if the bank will give you a list of these properties. They might even contact you when a property is added to the list.

Another great place to find a deal is through tax sales. Talk to the county, start with the county clerk, and see what properties have been foreclosed on because of delinquent taxes. Find out when the tax sale auction will be and go to it. If you buy a property at a tax sale, you'll need to provide a deposit onsite and will have to pay the balance within a couple of days.

There are other auction companies that sell homes and sometimes you can even find an estate sale. Step outside the box and discover unconventional ways to find good deals.

Once you've found some properties, choose the best few to actually look at. Remember, I said you'll need to look at 10 properties online or on paper before you go visit one, and you'll need to visit 10 properties before you put an offer on one. Again these are guidelines and not rules. So pick a few houses and schedule part of a day for you and your realtor to look at them. NOTE: If the property is for sale by owner, a foreclosure that the bank sent you, or a tax sale, the seller will most likely not pay your realtor a commission. If you want your realtor involved, you will likely have to come to an agreement on a commission that you'll pay him/her. Consider these costs in your numbers.

Step 4: Visit the property

Earlier, I told you that it was time to get busy. Well, now that you have a list of properties to look at, it's time to get busier. The goal is to evaluate a property as quickly as possible and move on. As a rule, I like to spend no more than 30 minutes in a property. I might come back and look at it again if I'm seriously considering making an offer. Here is a little checklist that I like to go through when I visit a property:

Clifford T. Wellman Jr.

1. Know the rental rate for similar properties, based on your market.
2. Determine the ARV - hopefully the realtor has an idea what it would sell for once it is fixed up.
3. Evaluate the exterior - roof, siding, windows, foundation, gutters - if any of these items needs to be addressed, you are talking about thousands of dollars in repairs. Take pictures so that you can remember the house when you are finalizing your numbers.
4. Evaluate the inside - bathroom(s), kitchens, living areas - if you have to do major repairs to bathrooms or kitchens, you are talking about thousands of dollars.
5. Evaluate the flooring - carpet, tile, wood, etc. - these are big ticket items. I can almost guarantee that you'll want to replace carpet, especially in a foreclosure.
6. Evaluate Utilities - plumbing, electric, water, sewer/septic, gas - if the electrical box has fuses, local ordinances might require that it be upgraded to circuit breakers. If the property has a well or septic system, you'll want the most recent inspection report (if you decide to put an offer on the property).
7. Evaluate the bedrooms - make sure all bedrooms have closets and meet the current standards for bedrooms. Nothing worse than buying a three bedroom house and finding out later that the 3rd bedroom doesn't count. That 3rd bedroom provides a lot of extra value to the house.
8. Evaluate the basement (if applicable) - is there evidence of water? If there is a sump-pump, does it work?
9. Evaluate the mechanical systems - water heater, water softener (if applicable), furnace/boiler, duct work and radiators, central air conditioning.
10. Evaluate the garage (if applicable) - including the driveway.
11. Evaluate the property - Does the property have adequate drainage? Does the land slope away from the house?

As you go through the house, jot down items that need repair and guestimate how much it will cost to repair. Take pictures as you feel necessary. By the end of your tour, you should have a pretty good idea how much it will cost to get the home up to the ARV.

Next, you will want to figure out your maximum purchase price. This number assumes that you are purchasing at a discount and takes into account repair costs and holding costs. You'll also want to calculate your estimated cash flow. Some houses generate cash flow. Others generate cash when you sell. Sometimes you can find both! The next couple tables show us how to calculate all these numbers.

Maximum Purchase Price	
Asking Price	$50,000
ARV	$70,000
75% of ARV	$52,500 (we buy at a discount)
Cost of Repairs	$20,000
Holding Costs	$ 4,200 ($700 x 6 months - from below)
Total Costs	$24,200
Max Purchase Price	$29,200 (75% of ARV - Total Costs)
Total Investment	$53,400 (Max Purch. Price + Total Costs)
Down Payment	$10,680 (20% down payment)
Mortgage Amount	$42,720

Holding Costs	
Mortgage Payment	$ 300
Insurance	$ 100
Taxes	$ 150
Total Holding Costs	$ 550 (add $150 for utilities = $700)
Vacancy	$ 40 (5% of Rent - see rent below)
Maintenance	$ 50
Total Expenses	$ 640

Cash Flow Numbers	
Monthly Rent	$ 800
Total Expenses	$ 640
Monthly Cash Flow	$ 160
Annual Cash Flow	$1,920

Clifford T. Wellman Jr.

When you first look at a property, you'll have to guess at the taxes and insurance, but with experience you should be able to get close. Your mortgage calculator app will help you determine the mortgage payment.

As you get better at doing these quick estimates, you'll figure out what numbers work best. With these numbers, I usually know before I leave the property whether I want to consider making an offer on the property or not. In this example, the first thing that we notice is that the monthly cash flow numbers don't meet our criteria of $200 per month. In order to hit $200 per month, we are going to have to reduce the mortgage payment by $40, or increase the monthly rent by $40. If your market can handle $40 more than your original assessment, then you're all set. A better option is to decrease the maximum purchase price to take into account this lower mortgage payment. A combination of both raising the rent and lowering the payment also works. You also might consider eliminating some of the repairs. Maybe you can paint the kitchen cabinets versus replacing them. Maybe you pick less expensive fixtures. Remember, you control how much money you spend on any given project. Another option is that you walk away from the property and wait to see if the asking price is lowered.

Step 5: Put an offer on the property

Now that you've visited several properties and narrowed down the list of properties that you want to make an offer on, it's time to make an offer or two. At this point, this process is actually going to cost you some money. First, once you get an accepted offer, you'll need to provide an earnest money deposit. Depending on the purchase price, this amount could be $500-1000 or more. You need to have this money available. Additionally, notice that I said that you don't pay this money until you get an accepted offer. This clause needs to be in your offer. You don't want to put out multiple offers and have to provide earnest money for each offer regardless if the offer is accepted or not. By the way, the earnest money deposit is applied to your down payment when you finally close the deal. This money is returned to you if the deal doesn't close because of any contingency failures.

"What is a contingency?" you ask.

When you make an offer, you always want to have contingencies that give you a way out of the deal. Example contingencies are:

- your ability to get financing
- a satisfactory property inspection - when you are first starting out, you will want to do a thorough inspection of the property before you buy it. Hire a property inspector who will go through and inspect the entire house including: roof, windows, siding, foundation, mechanical systems (furnace, A/C, water heater, etc), utility systems (electric, gas, water, etc). You can include virtually anything in your inspection. Your satisfaction is objective, meaning if you don't like something, then you walk away and you get your earnest money deposit back. Once I became experienced, I began performing my own inspections unless one of the major systems looked suspect, then I called in a professional.
- other contingencies - your realtor should be able to help provide you with a way out of any deal.
- MAKE SURE ALL CONTINGENCIES ARE SPELLED OUT IN THE PURCHASE AGREEMENT!

After you close a few deals, you'll realize that the purchase agreements that your realtor writes up are pretty standard. They become more complex when you start doing bigger deals that include multiple units. Anyway, work with your realtor when writing your first few offers.

Since we are already pre-approved for a loan, we know that the bank will most likely provide a loan for the majority of the purchase. However, we still need to come up with the remainder. There are a couple options for your down payment.

- cash - the bank likes this the best because it shows that you have some skin in the game.
- equity on another property - banks will sometimes accept equity on another property as down payment for your new property. However, most often the bank will want to refinance the first property in order to put both properties on a single loan. The main problem with this is

- that now there are two pieces of collateral on one loan and things get complicated when you try to sell one or both of the properties.
- borrow the down payment - in some cases a bank will allow you to borrow funds for your down payment. This option seems to be going away, but you can still find lenders who will consider it.
- seller financing - some banks will allow the seller to take a second position loan for the down payment. What this means is, the seller will lend you all or part of the down payment. In addition to paying the bank a monthly payment, you'll also be making a monthly payment to the seller until that down payment is completely paid off.

I'm sure there are other creative ways to come up with the down payment for your purchase. When you are just getting started, you might have to be the most creative. After you build a cash reserve, it will become easier.

"What if the bank won't finance the cost of the repairs?" you ask.

That is a good question. It is getting harder and harder to get a bank to finance the cost of repairs. Your relationship with the bank is probably the most important factor on whether they will do it or not. The other is the value of the property as is, and the cost of the repairs. When you are first getting started, unless you have a lot of cash available, it might be best to only tackle projects that don't require a lot of repairs. Keeping your first project simple will help with your sanity as well. Do you remember my first project? The one that almost kept me away from the real estate investing game?

One way to pay for repairs is through credit. If you have a big box store like Home Depot, Lowes, or Menards close to you, I would recommend getting a credit card from one or more of these stores. Most of these credit cards give you zero interest for 6-24 months, depending on the amount of your purchase. Just make sure that you pay off your balances before the zero interest rate term ends, otherwise you'll end up paying a lot of interest. Other credit cards can also be used for the cost of repairs. If you recall, one of the things that I mentioned about me in the beginning of this book was that I had good credit. Good credit will help you throughout your investment career. Protect your credit like you would your children. Check out the chapter on building credit later in this book for more information.

We've already talked about starting a company. It is a good idea to already have the company created before you place your offer and get pre-approved by the bank. That way the property can be purchased in the name of the company.

Step 6: Close on the property

Now that you have an accepted offer, it's time to finalize your loan with the bank (or credit union). Closing a loan will take 30-90 days, depending on the deal, the bank, and other circumstances. At this point, you'll have to provide to the bank a lot more details on your business and personal finances. The bank will want all your business and personal tax returns for the last three years. As a matter of fact, you'll have to continue to provide these each year to your bank(s), for as long as you have loans with them. You have to complete a loan application and most likely open a savings account with the bank. Part of the loan application is your Personal Financial Statement (PFS). As I said before, I like to keep my PFS current so that I can simply give the bank the most recent version. I also keep my PFS current so that I can track my own progress. Because you're buying the property through your company, you'll have to provide proof that the company exists. You'll have to provide the Articles of Organization (for Limited Liability Companies), FEIN (Federal Employer Identification Number) from the Internal Revenue Service (IRS), and an Operating Agreement (LLC). If you have an incorporated business, then you'll provide Articles of Incorporation and Company Bylaws instead of Articles of Organization and an Operating Agreement. Make sure that you look into the rules for creating these entities in your state before you get started. It is a good idea to hire a lawyer for the creation of your first company, but make sure you learn the process so that you can create the next company. Once you've created a business or two, you'll see that it's really not that hard and you can do it by yourself for a fraction of the cost.

If you are buying a home directly from the seller or it is a foreclosure, and you are not using a realtor, you'll want to work directly with a title company. Title companies will do all the heavy lifting and will make the process seamless. Some states require lawyers to be involved. Again, just make sure that you know what the rules are in your state. I highly recommend you use a realtor when buying your first property.

Clifford T. Wellman Jr.

When you go to your first closing, you will most likely be very nervous. You'll be sitting there with your realtor, a title agent, possibly your banker and sometimes with the seller. You'll be handing over a check for a lot of money to buy a piece of property that you are hoping you can rent or flip. I guarantee that you'll have knots in your stomach. But don't worry. This is the first step toward financial freedom. This is the first step toward realizing your dream!

Sit back, take a deep breath, and tell yourself that it's going to be okay.

Step 7: Perform repairs on the property

Okay, so now you've bought your first property. You just left the closing with less money and a set of keys to a property that you just bought. Hopefully you have a big smile on your face, because you realize that you are one step closer to achieving your dream.

It's time to get started on the repairs. Actually, once I've got an accepted offer and a final approval from the bank, I begin putting my plan together for the repair/rehab phase of this project. I will walk through the house and write down everything that needs to be repaired. I will identify any dependencies that exists. For instance, you'll want to paint everything before you put down flooring. I also identify which areas are outside my skill set and begin accepting bids from plumbers, electricians, roofers, and handymen. I like to know which contractors I will be hiring and I like to have them scheduled before I close on the property. That way we can hit the ground running.

When you are just getting started, you will want to take an active role in the repair phase of the project. You are going to want to watch how tasks are done, so that you can possibly handle them yourself in the future. This knowledge also helps you determine if a bid is realistic or not. A word of warning: You will discover that not all contractors are honest. Staying active on the project will help keep them honest. It is important early on to find contractors that you can trust. However, you don't want to become a micro-manager. Let them do their job, but if they aren't performing or aren't showing up, then it's time to let them go and find another. Never pay for a job upfront. It is fine to pay a deposit, but you need to hold back the majority of the money until the end. After a few projects you'll begin to see who is good and who is not. I mentioned earlier that your first property should probably have minimal repairs, because there will be less costs and less management necessary. You are new to the business and there will be a lot of moving parts for you to figure out.

When you hire contractors and receive bids from them, make sure that you get estimated completion dates and costs. There will almost always be unexpected costs and overruns. You have to plan for these overruns in your project plan.

Step 8: Rent the property

NOTE: This step only applies if you are holding the property to generate cash flow.

Once the property is ready to rent, it is time to find a tenant. I cannot express how important this phase is. Finding a good tenant can make or break the entire deal. Even though you are in a hurry to start making money, you need to be very diligent in selecting a tenant. Every potential tenant must complete an application. It is imperative that you get their driver's license number and social security number when the tenant actually signs a rental agreement. Make sure to take a photo copy of the potential tenants driver's license and social security card. You will need this information if you ever want to garnish wages or tax returns after an eviction.

On your application, you need to require at least five years of rental history and five years of work experience. If you are going to allow pets, then you'll need a section on the type of pet that the potential tenant has. For insurance purposes, you'll want to disallow certain types of dogs (such as a Pit Bull, Doberman, Rottweiler, etc). Every person I know that owns a pit bull says that they are harmless, and they probably are, but not all owners treat their pets properly. Certain breeds do have bad histories. Save yourself some trouble and simply disallow these breeds. Talk to your insurance agent about this. Some people don't like to allow pets and that is fine, but I see pets as another revenue stream. If I allow pets in a property, I charge additional pet rent. I also take a non-refundable pet deposit/fee that is used to offset the

Clifford T. Wellman Jr.

necessary cleaning you'll do when the tenant leaves. Pet rents range from $25-50 per pet per month and pet deposit/fees range from $100-$200. Be careful how you word such fees. Each state and county has different rules.

Earlier, we briefly talked about security deposits, but always take a security deposit equal to a month's rent or up to 1.5 times a month's rent. I don't care if you are renting to a family member, you should still take a security deposit.

When you get applications back, make sure that you call all rental references. Pay close attention to the landlords prior to their current landlord. A current landlord might give the potential tenant all sorts of praise if they are trying to get rid of a bad tenant. The previous landlord who has already gotten rid of them will most likely tell you the truth. As a landlord, don't ever give a positive reference for someone who doesn't deserve it. Always answer a new landlord's questions honestly even if you want the tenant out of your unit. It is also imperative that you verify employment history, as well as the potential tenant's current monthly gross income. If the potential tenant lies about anything, they should be disallowed immediately. Additionally, we require that a tenant earn a monthly gross income greater than or equal to three times the monthly rent. For instance, if the rent is $700, then the potential tenant must earn at least $2,100 in monthly gross income. If there are two applicants that are going to live in the house, we allow a combination of their income to be considered. Additionally, all tenants who are at least 18 years of age will be included on the rental agreement. All of these individuals are responsible for the payment of the entire rent, regardless of who leaves the property. Each one of these individuals must complete a rental application. Additionally, you can charge a non-refundable application fee. We charge $25-50 per person depending on the property. An application fee also helps to weed out those that aren't really serious about renting your property. Nothing is worse than spending time checking out a potential tenant, only to find out that they aren't interested in the property anymore.

So you've gone through your applications and found your top few potential tenants. Now it's time to choose which tenant you want in your property. Which one do you chose? This choice is a personal choice. Which one makes you feel the best? I like to choose married couples over a girlfriend and boyfriend combination. Why? Because a married couple is more likely to stay together than a girlfriend and boyfriend combo. I also like families over a group of unrelated people. Families tend to stick together, but the makeup of your tenants will be dependent on the market that you are in. NEVER, NEVER, NEVER choose a tenant based on race or sex, or any other protected class. The last thing you need is a lawsuit. The one thing you CAN discriminate against is criminals. We never allow Felons or Sex Offenders in any of our properties. This is increasingly more important when you have an apartment complex or mobile home park. If you have a sex offender in your complex, this will keep families and other individuals away from your complex. Your potential tenant base will be drastically reduced. There are several free ways to do a background check on individuals. Also, you can choose to perform credit checks on a potential tenant, but we never do. Most tenants tend to have poor credit, so it just doesn't make financial sense to waste money on a credit check when you almost always know that their credit will be poor.

Once you've selected a tenant and they've accepted, it's time to sign a rental agreement. It is a good idea to have a lawyer review your rental agreement. If your realtor is also an investor, he/she will most likely have an agreement that you can modify. You can find samples online almost anywhere. Any rental agreement should include the rent amount, the security deposit amount, and a late fee amount and schedule. Make sure your late fees are in line with your local rules. We charge a $25 late fee on the 2nd day of the month if the rent is not paid by the 1st of the month. We charge an additional $5 every day the tenant is late. This ensures that the tenant pay the rent as soon as possible. As I said earlier, we also start the eviction process if rent is not paid on time. We'll go into that in further detail in the next step.

Before the tenant moves in, you need to perform a walkthrough of the property and document the current condition of everything. We like to do the walkthrough with the tenant when we sign the rental agreement and have them sign the property assessment checklist. This ensures that they are aware of the current condition of the property. If there is a chip from the paint in the living room we write it down. This may seem silly to include something that minor, but it really helps to resolve disputes later on when you deduct money from the tenant's security deposit.

Clifford T. Wellman Jr.

Step 9: Manage the property

Whew, so now you have a tenant in your rental property. You are collecting rent every month on time and everything is awesome. So what's next? Well, there are a few things that can happen:

- things keep rolling as smooth as ever - yay!
- the tenant reports a problem - it's time to either go and fix it or call a contractor to fix it. Remember when I was showing you the cash flow calculation numbers and I included a line item for *maintenance*? Yep, every month that the rent is paid, put this maintenance amount into a side account for future repairs. So it's been four months that you've collected rent on time and you've put aside $200 ($50 x 4 months). Then the tenant calls and says that the bathroom faucet is leaking slightly. You go over and determine that you need to replace it. If you can fix it, then you buy a faucet for $75 and spend an hour repairing the faucet. Fortunately, you had $200 set aside for this. Well, let's say that you don't have the experience repairing a faucet and you have to call a plumber. The plumber is going to charge you $150 to install your $75 faucet. Now your cost is $225. Fortunately, you put aside $200 already and will only be out of pocket $25, which you'll get back next month when the tenant pays rent again.
- the tenant quits paying rent - Crap! Okay, so it's the second of the month and the tenant hasn't paid the rent. Send the tenant a Demand for Possession letter. This letter tells the tenant that they have seven days to pay or get out. Maybe the tenant simply forgot and sends the rent in before the seven days are up. But maybe they don't. Now it's time to get serious and get your lawyer involved. I'm not going to go through the details of this process in this book, because every state has a different process. So make sure you know what process you need to go through to evict a tenant. Be aware of your own state and local landlord/tenant laws and rules.
- the tenant decides to leave in the middle of the night and they did a ton of damage - Crap! Before you do anything, take pictures of everything. Make sure there is a date stamp on the pictures. You have their social security number, so you can file a lawsuit and

hopefully get a judgment for all of the costs of the repairs. One thing that you need to understand is that just because you have a judgment, doesn't mean you have the money. You will most likely have to garnish the tenant's wages and tax returns.

- the tenant's lease is up and they don't want to renew. Once they've vacated the property, you need to assess the property once again. We have a move-in/move-out checklist that we use to compare the condition of the property when the tenant moved in to the condition when they moved out. If there is damage in excess of normal wear and tear, then we charge the tenant for these damages. If the damages are less than the security deposit, then we send them the balance. If the damages exceed the amount of the security deposit, then we may possibly sue for damages.

Well, congratulations! You own your first property and are collecting cash flow each month. It's time to do it again! Wash, rinse and repeat!

Building your credit score

In the previous chapter, I mentioned your credit report. When you are just starting out, if you've never had a loan or a credit card, you might not actually have any credit. This can be a problem for banks and other lenders. They want to see that you have made your payments in the past. Without credit, you are going to find it difficult to get a loan on your first property. So find some free credit report site (like www.creditkarma.com) and find out what your credit score is. If you don't have a credit score, there are a few ways to get one established.

- open a credit card - credit card companies are more likely to give you a little credit when getting started. All you need is $500 in credit to get started. Open the card and use the card to purchase your gas for your car. Don't use it for anything else at this point. Make sure to pay off the credit card completely each month. After a few months, you'll start seeing that you have a credit score. Most credit card companies report to the three main credit bureaus once a month.
- go to a bank and ask for a small loan of $500-1000. You might be able to get a small loan like this without any collateral. Put the money into a side account and setup an automatic payment from that account to pay the loan over a period of 6-12 months. Make sure the bank will be reporting your activity to the credit bureaus.
- buy a car and finance it - I know that I said it was a bad idea to finance an asset that doesn't generate cash flow, but banks are more likely to give you a loan if there is collateral tied to it. This type of loan will help you build credit.

Get creative. Tell your bank that you are trying to build your credit. They might be interested in helping you, especially if they know that they will be seeing more of you in the future as you build your business.

If you get your credit report back and your credit score is below 600, then you need to drill into your credit report and see what is going on. A credit score of 650 isn't too bad, but if you can get it into the 700's, you'll look better to a lending institution. Sites like www.creditkarma.com show you the reasons why your credit score is low. There are even "what-if" calculators that help you figure out how to improve your credit. There are three categories that have a high impact on your credit score.

- Derogatory Marks
- Credit Card Balances
- Payment History

Derogatory Marks

If you have bad marks on your credit report, you need to fix them. For instance, if you have some old debt that you never paid back, and for whatever reason you decided not to pay it, and now it's in collections, it's time to man up (or woman up) and pay it off. These types of things will haunt you forever. There are ways to dispute a bad mark, but if you owe the debt, you need to pay the debt. Tax liens, bankruptcies or civil judgments will also negatively affect your credit score.

Credit Card Balances

If your credit report shows that your credit card balances are too high compared to your total credit amount, then you need to do something to decrease that ratio. For instance, most credit bureaus want to see less than 30% credit card utilization. If you have $10,000 of total credit and have a $4,000 balance, then you are at 40% utilization and they don't like that. Pay $1,000 or more and get that percent down below 30%. Interestingly, you can open a new credit card for $5,000 of credit and not pay the $1,000 that I just mentioned, and now your ratio is 26.7%. Here's the math:

Total Credit : $15,000 (original $10,000 + new $5,000)
Credit Balance: $4,000
Credit Ratio: $4,000 ÷ $15,000 = 26.7%

Don't get carried away with credit cards. Too many can be a bad thing, especially if you use them and hold balances on them.

Clifford T. Wellman Jr.

Payment History

You want to make sure that all of your loan and credit card payments are ALWAYS made on time and never late. Utility companies will also report to credit agencies. Every time you're late, you get a ding! Too many dings and your credit score goes down. It is a good idea to do your best to pay all of your bills on time.

Balance Sheets

Earlier in the book I talked about creating a balance sheet. I recommend purchasing a bookkeeping software package to help manage your finances. I use QuickBooks and it does pretty much everything I need. There are more expensive and more elaborate products out there. You just need to figure out what best meets your needs.

A balance sheet provides a comparison between Assets and Liabilities and Capital. Assets show up on the left side (the debit side) and liabilities and capital show up on the right side (the credit side).

This table provides a few examples of each:

Income Generating Assets	Liabilities
Real Estate	Mortgage
Stocks & Bonds	Loans on Cars, Boats, etc.
Notes	Credit Cards
Intellectual Property	

Income Generating Assets

Real Estate - this would be any rental real estate that generates income.

Stocks & Bonds - these provide a periodic dividend income.

Notes - this is a loan that you hold for someone else that generates interest income.

Intellectual Property - these are things like patents, trade names, franchises, copyrights, and trademarks.

There are other assets that could qualify as income generating assets.

Liabilities

Mortgage - a loan on a property is an expense that takes money out of your pocket.

Loans - cars, boats, and other toys have an expense that takes money out of your pocket.

Credit Cards - similar to mortgages and loans.

Conclusion

Assets are found on the left side of a Balance Sheet, generate income, and put money in your pocket. *Liabilities* are found on the right side of a Balance Sheet and have an associated expense that takes money out of your pocket. The left side of the Balance Sheet, where the Assets go, is called the Debit side. The right side of the Balance Sheet, where the Liabilities and Capital go, is called the Credit side.

Being Rich versus Wealthy

As you build your business, you inch closer to your goal and the value of your assets is piling up. Actually, there is a real good chance that before you reach your goal, you have over $1,000,000 in assets. If you have a million in assets, does that make you a millionaire? No, not quite. There are three different $1,000,000 thresholds.

- Buy a million
- Own a million
- Make a million

Buy a million

This means that you have bought over $1,000,000 in assets. At this point, you are not necessarily a millionaire. Let's say you bought your 20 rental properties that are valued at $50,000 each. At that point, you have $1,000,000 in assets. However, since you most likely have mortgages on all of them, you aren't a millionaire yet. Let's say on average you owe $30,000 on each house, so you have $600,000 in liabilities. Your net worth is $400,000 (assets - liabilities). That's good, but you're not a millionaire. At this point you are also making about $4,000 each month in cash flow, which is about $48,000 annually. That is nice passive income, but as you know, you are most likely still living month to month.

Own a million

Let's forward the clock to a time when you have 40 rental properties, each worth $50,000. You now have $2,000,000 in assets. For each of these properties you have $25,000 in debt. That is $1,000,000 in liabilities. At this point your net worth is now $1,000,000 (assets - liabilities). You are officially a millionaire on paper. The down side is, you still might not have a lot of cash in the bank or in your pocket. You definitely should have enough cash flow to pay all your bills and live comfortably, but if you are still growing your business, then you aren't totally out of the woods yet. At this point you are probably making close to $10,000 a month or $120,000 in annual cash flow. Things are a lot smoother and hopefully you're not living month to month. You will have saved some money for emergencies, but by no means do you feel rich. At this point, you have moved away from single unit purchases and are working on small multi-unit properties like duplexes, triplexes, and quads.

Make a million

Now let's talk about making a million. In order to make $1,000,000 annually in cash flow, you need to make just about $84,000 a month in passive income. This means that you've increased your holdings by about 8 times what it was in the *Own a million* section. You should have between 300-400 units. At this point, you should have significant savings and ample cash flow to do whatever it is that you want to do. You are relying on your team to keep the train on the rails. Your primary job should be high level management and analysis of cash flow. You are primarily focused on business development and acquisitions. You are no longer focusing on properties that are less than 10-20 units. You are buying larger apartment complexes and other multi-unit properties.

The title of this chapter is *Being Rich versus Wealthy*. The main difference is that if you are rich, you have a lot of cash. If you are wealthy, you have a lot of cash flow (and probably a lot of cash). Our goal should be to obtain the status of being wealthy. Cash flow should be a continuous stream of cash for eternity.

Managing Risk

We have all probably heard someone tell us that something was risky. Maybe it was investing in the stock market. Maybe it was investing in real estate. Maybe it was creating a business. All of these things can be risky, and all of these things can be relatively safe. The difference is how you educate yourself. For instance, it would be risky to take $10,000 and buy stock in a particular company that you know absolutely nothing about. You actually might have better odds at winning black jack or roulette. My point is that it is a gamble to invest in a stock that you know nothing about. It is also a gamble to buy a house that is in a market that you know nothing about. If you don't know what property values or what rental rates are in a particular market, then you have no business investing in those markets. It is risky to invest in things you know nothing about.

"But my brother-in-law is in real estate," you say. OR

"My uncle told me that ABC stock was going to go up," you say.

Great, go ahead and listen to these people, but it is still risky. You are relying solely on <u>their</u> experience and education to make you money. They may have done well in the past, or maybe not, but if you leave it up to them, then you might as well take your money to Vegas. Okay, I realize that I might be acting a little harshly, but the point is that if you are going to invest, you need to educate yourself first.

Education

Education can come in many forms. You can go to college, you can take a course, you can read a book, or watch a video. I'm sure there are lots of other ways to educate yourself. Prior to getting started in real estate investing, my wife and I both held Bachelor degrees from a University. We were educated and well rounded according to university standards, but neither of us knew anything about rental real estate. When we finally decided to get into the rental real estate investing game, we took it upon ourselves to get an education specifically in real estate. We read countless books, listened to audio tapes, and watched videos. We even took courses and workshops. To be honest, we probably spent the equivalent amount that we would have spent on a Masters degree. But we didn't stop there. Even today, I continually read and learn about real estate and other investment strategies.

Know your market

After educating yourself on general studies in real estate, it is time to educate yourself on your market. You must know what houses are being bought and sold for in your market. You must know what rental rates you can get. You must know the local landlord/tenant rules. You must know what kinds of properties lending institutions are lending on. You must know which neighborhoods to look for houses in, and which neighborhoods to stay away from.

Patience and Diligence

After you've educated yourself, you need to exercise patience. Don't go out and buy the first home you look at. Take your time and find the right deal, not just any deal. Do your due diligence and make sure that the deal you are looking at truly is the right deal.

Control

Risk Management is all about control. You control at what price you buy a property. You control at what amount you rent a property. If the property doesn't meet your criteria, then you don't buy it. The house you're looking at right now isn't the only house out there. If you're not sure if you should buy a particular property, say a little prayer to God and wait for an answer.

Conclusion

Educate yourself. Know your market. Be patient and diligent. Be in control!

Building a Team

I have already told you that you can't go it alone. You need a team of good people around you to be successful in the rental real estate game. Here is a list of people that you'll need on the team. They aren't listed in order of importance, but more in order of who you'll need first.

- Realtor
- Banker
- Accountant
- Lawyer
- Insurance Agent
- Maintenance
- Management

Realtor

A good realtor is the first team member that you're going to find. There are two types of realtors. Those who invest and those who don't. For the most part, you want to avoid a realtor who doesn't invest. You need a realtor who can go into a property and tell you what it could rent for, what the ARV (After Repair Value) is, and how much you are going to spend on repairs. Eventually, you'll be able to come up with these numbers yourself, but in the beginning you'll need help and later on you'll want a sounding board. If you're lucky, like I was, you build a friendship that will last. A good realtor will bring properties to you, that meet your criteria. He/she may also bring you properties that you didn't know you were looking for. You might think that a realtor who invests doesn't want competition. If that is the case, then you don't want that realtor, because he's not going to help you. A good realtor who invests won't be afraid of your competition, he'll help you build your portfolio and be happy to see you grow. There is a lot of real estate out there. No one person can buy them all. It's easy to share and more fun when you're not out there doing it alone. By the way, you should only have ONE realtor per area where you are investing. Find one and be loyal to them, as long as they are loyal to you.

Clifford T. Wellman Jr.

Banker

There are a few things that you are looking for in a banker. First, I have already said that I like small local banks and credit unions. These bankers will develop personal relationships with you. Large banks will only see you as a bunch of numbers. As you build relationships, local bankers will see what you're doing in the community and they'll see the condition of your properties. The second thing you are looking for is a banker who truly has his/her finger on the pulse of the community. They'll know what properties are needed and what types are saturated. For instance, I have a banker friend who has recommended that I buy storage unit properties in my area. They are booming right now. Every time we sit down to close a loan, we spend more time on ideas for the next property. A good banker will act as a sounding board as well. Third, you're looking for a banker that will lend on the properties that interested you. In a previous chapter, I mentioned that several banks weren't interested in lending on mobile home parks because they had bad experiences in the past. That's okay, they might be interested in storage units. There are other banks out there that will lend you money. Having relationships with multiple banks is incredibly important.

Accountant

As is the case with all of the members of your team, your accountant should either be an investor or have a lot of clients that invest in rental real estate (or whatever other business you are involved in). They must have the expertise to make sure you pay the least amount of taxes that the government allows. Reducing your tax burden is their number one responsibility. A secondary requirement is to have an accountant that can help you evaluate various business opportunities. As I said early, I don't just meet with my accountant during tax season. We talk throughout the year. When my banker told me that I should invest in storage units, I ran the idea by my accountant. He loved the idea as well. So I'm in the process of shopping around for storage unit properties.

Bookkeeper

A bookkeeper is used to help run the daily financial business of paying bills and collecting rents. When you first get started, you'll do all of the bookkeeping yourself. Buy an accounting package, like QuickBooks, and get started. As you grow, you'll find more and more of your time consumed by collecting rents and paying bills. Your goal is to be retired, so find a trustworthy bookkeeper who will take care of these tasks. However, it is very important that you stay on top of the money going in and out of your accounts. Set up a system that allows you to manage at a high level, with weekly or monthly reports. I have a friend who spends his winters sailing around on his catamaran in the Bahamas. He has a bookkeeper who takes care of all the day-to-day tasks and he just reads reports. If there is ever an anomaly, he gets in touch with his bookkeeper.

Lawyer

A lawyer becomes more important as you grow. Depending on your area, you may need a lawyer to deal with evictions. I know that in some counties where we have properties, we have to have a lawyer to do an eviction. In other counties, we don't. You'll have to figure out at what point you need one. In some areas, lawyers are also needed when you buy and sell properties. In Michigan, we have title companies for closings, but in other states they use lawyers. Know the rules in your area. Another use for your lawyer is to help you put together a will and a trust. By the way, we actually use multiple lawyers. You'll want your eviction lawyers to be local to your properties. Your will and trust lawyer can be wherever you decide.

Insurance Agent

An insurance agent will be needed when you buy your first property, but they really start to become important when you begin to grow. As I said earlier, an insurance agent will help you save money by bundling policies and will help you protect your assets through multiple levels of insurance. I like to have just one insurance agent regardless of how many locations I have, but you might decide to go a different route.

Clifford T. Wellman Jr.

Maintenance

Maintenance is a tricky beast. You'll need many people for various tasks. You'll need different people to do different things. Sometimes a handyman can do it all, but sometimes you need multiple people to get the job done in a timely manner. Getting a good handyman is your first task. Get one who is reasonably priced who can do almost every task listed below. Eventually you'll need specialized personnel as well.

- Plumbing
- Electrical
- Heating and Cooling
- Carpentry
- Drywall
- Roofing
- Siding & Windows
- Foundation and Excavating
- Landscaping
- Flooring
- Painting
- Lawn care (mowing)
- Snow removal

When you are first getting started, I recommend you learn to do all of the maintenance tasks yourselves. This will give you the skills to keep your maintenance contractors honest. As you grow your business, you will want and need to rely on several others. Of primary importance is to have a local handyman who can do many different tasks.

Property Management

As you grow, you will come to find out that your property manager(s) is the most important member of your team. As I said before, my friend spends his winter sailing his boat in warm waters, thousands of miles from his properties. He couldn't do that without good property managers. Your property manager(s) will make sure that all of your properties are full. They will coordinate maintenance and repairs. They will deal with collections and evictions. This person is basically doing all of the work that you used to do. They are the ones that are allowing you to stay retired. If you extend your investment dealing beyond rental properties, you'll need managers for other endeavors like running your manufacturing business, your restaurants, your golf courses, etc. The only thing that will limit you, is your imagination.

Where are you?

So where are you in your path toward retirement? Many people work 40 hours a week at a job that they hopefully like. If their employer provides benefits, they invest in a 401k and have access to insurance. Most of these people live paycheck to paycheck and are counting on their 401k and social security to provide their retirement income and Medicare to provide health insurance. Unfortunately, almost none of these people will retire early and will have to work well into their 60s and possibly 70s.

There are four levels or stations in our investment life. Each level provides different levels of financial freedom. The levels are:

- Employee
- Self Employed or Small Business
- Large Business
- Investor

Employee

An employee is someone who is employed by a business, school, or government agency. This person could be paid hourly or could be paid straight salary. Some of these employees will receive an insurance package that is partially paid for by the employer. They may have access to a 401k or 403b retirement account. Most likely these businesses no longer pay a pension, but it is still possible. Some of these employees might receive other perks like stock options, automobile access, cell phone, etc. This group of people includes all employees from a cashier at a grocery store, all the way to a CEO of a Fortune 500 company. Regardless of the job, they are dependent on their employer to continue to pay them. Their employer is responsible for paying part of their social security and Medicare taxes. All the money that these people are paid falls into the *earned income* bucket. Earned income is taxed at a higher rate than passive income.

Self Employed or Small Business

This level includes small businesses that employ less than five hundred employees. It also includes those that are self-employed, such as doctors, lawyers, CPAs, software consultants, building contractors, etc. Self-employed people get paid only as long as they continue to work. These people potentially make more money than someone in the *Employee* level, but their income is still dependant on their own ability to work. One negative as a small business or self-employed person, is that they are responsible for the employee portion as well as the business portion of the social security and Medicare taxes. As a result, a person at this level will end up paying even more taxes than a person at the *Employee* level. A small business owner will likely work more hours than an employee. The value of the business in this level might be completely dependent on the owner, and therefore be worthless without the owners participation. This is definitely the case in regards to a self-employed person. Once you stop working, there no longer is an income stream.

As the owner of a small business, if you are able to structure the business in such a way that you are not required to work the business daily, than you are moving in the direction of the *Large Business* level. In my opinion, the biggest differentiator between the *Small Business* level and the *Large Business* level is how dependent the business is on its owner for day-to-day operations. When you first start your small business, you will be required to work extra hours to keep it going, but as your business grows you'll be forced to delegate job responsibilities to others. After all, there are only so many hours in the day, and you need to sleep sometime. One advantage of a small business is that you can begin to deduct certain expenses to reduce earned income.

Large Business

A large business is one that employs five hundred employees or more, but the most important aspect of being at this level is the amount of work that must be done to receive a paycheck. As the owner of a large business, you might earn a salary as the CEO or President, but you'll also earn passive income in the form of the business profit. **NOTE: in the case mentioned here, you would**

Clifford T. Wellman Jr.

be in both the *Employee* level and the *Large Business* level. You'll receive earned income as an employee and passive income as the business owner. As a large business, you'll be able to take advantage of many of the tax laws that exist to help reduce the taxes on business income. These tax laws exist to encourage businesses to employee people. As a business owner, you'll pay taxes at the lower rate associated with passive income. Obviously, as the CEO, you'll still pay taxes at the rate associated with earned income. Being the business owner provides additional freedoms that aren't available at the *Employee* and *Small Business* levels. As a large business owner, you could hire a CEO to take over your job responsibilities and continue to receive passive income from the business.

Investor

A person at this level is receiving money only in the form of passive income. Most of this book covers passive income received from rental real estate. This is the primary source of my income, but rental real estate doesn't have to be the only means for achieving passive income. Review the partial list that we talked about earlier in the chapter on Passive Income for more ideas. As an investor, you'll pay the lowest tax rate because all of your income will fall into the passive income area. Additionally, you'll create Limited Liability Companies (LLC) to hold all of your investments. These LLCs will allow you to reduce your taxable income by deducting certain expenses from your gross revenues. It is at this level that you'll receive access to the vast majority of the tax laws that were created for people at this level. Again, the reason for this is that people at this level create jobs and grow the economy. At this level, you will have finally achieved true financial freedom.

Conclusion

A person can exist in all four of these categories simultaneously. I'm sure you can think of examples of how this is true. I was at the *Employee* level for nine years before I started doing software consulting on the side. At that point, I was in the *Employee* level and *Small Business* (Self-Employed) level. Then when I began investing in real estate, I added the *Investor* level. At some point I stopped working as an employee and was only at the *Self-Employed* and *Investor* levels. When I finally built up real estate assets that generated enough passive income to pay all the bills, I stopped doing software consulting and focused strictly on the *Investor* level. That is the moment that I retired. When I tell people that I've retired, some people laugh. They say something like, "You work all the time. How do you consider yourself retired?" My response is, "Any work that I do is in the form of adding assets to my portfolio so that I can continue to increase my passive income. I increase my means so that I can do the things that I want to do, when I want to do them." I spend my days looking for real estate deals or business deals. I help my wife create companies. I also spend a lot of time writing. I never intending to become an author, but here I am. The book that you are reading is the third book that I have published. I am actively working on a fourth book and have another 5-10 waiting to be written. Writing might seem like work, but I don't think of it like that. I really enjoy telling a story or sharing knowledge with people like yourself.

List of my books

The Road to Revelation - The Beginning
The Road to Revelation - World at War
The Road to Revelation - Darkness Falls (coming in 2019)
The Road to Revelation - Life and Death (coming in 2020 or sooner)
Three other books in the Road to Revelation series (coming after 2020)

Charity

Fifty percent of the income generated by the books in The Road to Revelation series is going to charity. Currently, I give to Hospice of Michigan, St. Jude Children's Hospital, St. Vincent DePaul, and other local charities. I am in the process of creating a scholarship in the name of my father. My family currently holds one annual event to raise funds for this scholarship.

I believe that as we increase our means, we should also increase our charity. Even while in the *Employee* level, find a way to give. Things can be tight when you're living in the *Employee* level, but it doesn't always have to be in the form of money. Maybe give some of your time as well.

Parting words

I tried to do my best to help guide you through the process of purchasing rental real estate for the purpose of generating passive income. I hope that you have learned a few things in these past 100 pages or so. Looking back on my history, I wish that I had started investing sooner in life. That is one wish that I have for you as well.

Start Now!

Don't let your fear stop you from achieving your dreams. Don't let the negativity of others stop you either. Don't do it for the money. I know that might sound strange, but there are more important things than money.

"Yeah, sure, now that you're retired, money doesn't matter!" you say in a sarcastic tone.

I learned that money wasn't the most important thing many years before I started investing in real estate. As a matter of fact, I learned it when I got fired from my job as Director of Internet Development. There is no amount of money that would have made me happy at that job. I told you that I got fired because my boss and I just didn't get along, and that is true. I wasn't happy in the cut-throat corporate environment that I was in, but I loved the money. I had spent the previous 10-12 years doing everything in my power to move up the corporate ladder, only to find out that moving up wasn't what I really wanted.

What I really wanted was to be free. To be free financially. To be free to do the things that I wanted to do. To be free to live the life that I always dreamed of. It was after I made the choice to be free, that I began to find true financial success. Before that, I was just another cog in the machine.

I wish you the best in your future real estate investing journey.

Thank you

Thank you for reading my book. I really hope that you enjoyed it. If you did, I would appreciate it if you could give this book a five star review on Amazon and Goodreads. Thanks again!

If you like this book I have two more coming soon:

- How to Buy and Sell Real Estate - An Investor's Guide (coming soon)
- Property Management Simplified (coming in 2020)

Please follow me on Social Media:

Website: http://www.cliffwellman.com

Facebook: https://www.facebook.com/CliffWellmanAuthor

For The Road to Revelation specific information

Website: http://www.TheRoadToRevelation.com

Facebook: https://www.facebook.com/TheRoadToRev

Twitter: https://www.twitter.com/RoadRevelation

Subscribe to newsletter: http://bit.ly/2VKM26l

www.ingramcontent.com/pod-product-compliance
Lightning Source LLC
Chambersburg PA
CBHW021445210526
45463CB00002B/640